lives in West London and lectures in English a Greenwich University. She has contributed short stories to women's magazines and anthologies such as *The Plot Against Mary* (The Women's Press, 1992) and . . . *And a Happy New Year!* (The Women's Press, 1993). She has won a number of literary awards and has just completed her first novel, *A Matter of Madness*.

Marijke Woolsey was born in North London in 1963. She divides her time between editing, teaching creative writing for Hammersmith and Fulham Adult Education, raising two children, reading through Jonathan Cape's 'slush pile' and trying to find time to write. So far she has had several short stories published including pieces in the anthologies she co-edited, *The Man Who Loved Presents* (The Women's Press, 1991), *The Plot Against Mary* (The Women's Press, 1992), and . . . *And a Happy New Year!* (The Women's Press, 1993). She has also completed three novels, the first of which was shortlisted for the Betty Trask Award.

Judith Arcana is the author of *Our Mothers' Daughters* (The Women's Press, 1981) and *Every Mother's Son* (The Women's Press, 1983). She is professor of Literature and Women's Studies at The Graduate School of the Union Institute in the United States.

Dear Mother...

An Anthology of Women Writing to or about their Mothers

Marijke Woolsey and Susan King, editors

Introduced by Judith Arcana

First published by The Women's Press Ltd, 1994
A member of the Namara Group
34 Great Sutton Street, London EC1V 0DX

Reprinted 1997

British Library Cataloguing-in-Publication Data
A catalogue record for this book is available from the British Library

ISBN 0 7043 4530 7

Phototypeset in Bembo by Intype, London
Printed and bound in Great Britain by
Cox & Wyman Ltd, Reading, Berks

ACKNOWLEDGEMENTS

The editors would like to thank Kathy Gale at The Women's Press for her guidance, support and sense of humour in times of crisis; Haringey and Islington libraries for their persistence and dedication in locating the material we were searching for; and all the writers, publishers and agents who worked with us to make this anthology possible.

PERMISSIONS

The editors would like to thank the following:

Mary Daly, for an extract from *Outercourse/The Be-Dazzling Voyage/Containing Recollections from My Log-book of a Radical Feminist Philosopher/(Be-ing an Account of My Time/Space Travels and Ideas – Then, Again, Now and How)*. Copyright © Mary Daly, 1992.

A M Heath and Company Ltd, for an extract from *I Knew a Phoenix*, copyright © May Sarton, 1954, 1956, 1959; and for permission to reprint 'Crescent moon like a canoe', copyright © Marge Piercy and Middlemarsh Inc, 1979, 1980.

Little, Brown and Company Ltd, for an extract from *Our Kate*. Copyright © Catherine Cookson, 1969.

Karen Payne, for an extract from *Between Ourselves*:

CONTENTS

To Paula and all other daughters who have struggled to be good mothers.

INTRODUCTION

The editors of *Dear Mother . . .*, fully aware of the hard and painful struggle between so many mothers and daughters, have chosen to make a book that celebrates the ways mothers and daughters can be together. They have collected classic writing on the mother/daughter relationship, and they offer this collection as a gift to us all, daughters of our mothers.

They chose to make a book that will raise our spirits and encourage us, urging us toward the under-standing and compassion we need when we seek the truth of our mothers' lives – and our own – as we grow in consciousness as women.

The themes of mother/daughter relationship fill these pages, presented by writers with the skill and delicacy of women in love. Beginning in 'A Letter from Kate to her mother, Teresa', we read the affec-tionate gratitude of a daughter who has taken years to see, to know, and to understand what she has learned from her mother, a woman apparently so different from herself.

An excerpt from Audre Lorde's biomythography, *Zami*, describes the deep sexual connection between women who are mother and daughter. Lorde shows us here how it is that our mothers are the first women we love. George Sand and Sylvia Plath's letters are evidence of the passion of the mother/daughter bond from different times, different places. Virginia Woolf too explains that our mothers stand at the centre of our lives, especially in our childhood, and Maya Angelou's memoir offers a grandmother who is as solid in that centre as the Rock of Ages.

Woolf, Lorde, and Marilyn French demonstrate the ability of the daughter to create the mother's character with the truth of art, writing out of life – a skill born in love. French writes too of the shock of similarity between mother and daughter, and of the daughter's recognition that her mother has become *an old woman*.

Stephanie Dowrick writes about the interposition of 'Dad' between mother and daughter, the effect of the presence of this powerful male figure, in metaphor and reality, on the mother/daughter relationship. Mary Daly writes of her great good fortune in knowing she is exactly what her mother wanted: one child, and that child a daughter.

The 'Indian woman' who speaks through Rachel Barton has been blessed with what Adrienne Rich showed us years ago is every daughter's dream: the mother who is a saviour, who rescues her daughter from horror and degradation, literally carrying her off to freedom and safety. And Maya Angelou gives us a hero-mother who is a variation on that theme: appearing from nowhere, taking her daughter off to a world she never imagined, protecting her in that unknown new world.

The complement, women's dreams of rescuing our mothers and bringing them to the recognition and position they deserve, is Marge Piercy's subject. She makes the link between contemporary women's movements for liberation and our mothers' movement toward the fulfilment too few of them came near.

Catherine Cookson's memoir is a fine lesson in clarity of understanding. Here is a mother who has hurt her daughter out of the misery of the mother's own life – misery for which she can see no cure, no hope, no correction – but whose daughter sees so clearly that she cares for her ageing mother with vigour and pleasure.

May Sarton enlarges upon Cookson's theme, showing us the desperate importance of knowing our mothers in terms of their own lives, before we were their daughters, before they were anyone's mothers. And Alice Walker widens this theme, focusing on the need of women in marginalised, oppressed and despised groups, especially Black women, to find the motherroot in the gardens of our lives. Claiming the generations of women who've gone before us as our mothers and grandmothers, she warns us that, lacking knowledge of the mothers' lives, we are cut off from our roots. Without knowledge of our mothers we are lost, and cannot fully be ourselves.

* * *

The mother/daughter relationship is central to our lives as women and to the history of all women. This collection holds some of the crucial knowledge of that history.

Judith Arcana, 1993

A LETTER FROM KATE
TO HER MOTHER, TERESA

14 October 1977

Dearest Mumma,

Many many thanks for your loving letter, and for your gift, which touched me very much indeed. I could just imagine you fretting around the shops, looking for something to cheer me, and that moved me lots and lots. It duly hangs upon my 'study' (grand, eh!) wall, opposite my desk, there for when I'm feeling totally devoid of inspiration, chewing my pencil and thinking perhaps I should take up charring instead. Don't worry about not being able to get that picture you wanted for me, it's the thought that counts, and yours I know are always dear and loving.

I'm feeling all soft and gooey tonight, very peaceful and contented. I've been reading through all my old letters, diaries and things, and it is very good to see how much I've changed, how far I've moved from all the fears and hangups that used to beset me. At times I was also a self-indulgent bitch, but I guess I had to go through all that, work through all the mud and anger, to finally come out, something like shining, on top.

And feeling especially loving towards you; reading all your old letters, remembering all the hurts and misunderstandings we had, and you – and I – desperately trying to make sense of it all. Your love still and always there, even the times I was furthest from you, and the times I hit out and hurt.

And now? So much has changed between us these past two years. I feel our relationship has become very good and strong again, and I love you very much. As for your love, it is an anchor for me, keeps me warm and brave when the going gets tough. I think what we went through was indeed a lot to do just with the simple process of growing up; me having to pull away in order to come back, and you, as mother having to let me go in order for that coming back. We have both changed and adapted, and now I feel we are friends as well as mother and daughter – and that is something precious and, I think, quite rare. All my friends envy our relationship, you know, and are very fond of you, admire you a lot, think you a great tough soft lady, gutsy and fun, big and brave . . . all of which you are! I am as proud of you as you are of me.

Now I'm older I can better understand how difficult it must have been for you at times; to let your child kick out and rebel, and make mistakes and get hurt a lot at times, but all the experience I've had has made me the person I now am, understanding more and trying to put all that experience to good use with my writing. I think one of the break points was when you realised my politics and life-style didn't mean I'd one day come crawling home with three illegitimate children/VD/heroin marks on my arm/a wooden leg/two syphilitic parrots and three buckets of dung and call it 'Art' . . . though at times you may have been right to worry!

What seems so good to me now is how both our ideas have changed, it's not one-sided, and there are many things we can talk and care about and share, where once there would only have been explosions. Women's Liberation, and my not particularly wanting to get married, etcetera – now you see I can in fact take care of myself, you don't have to act the moralist, and now I'm older and wiser I can also see where my idealism did put me at risk. With society as sexist as it is, and men as piggish as they often can be, I can now understand how hard it has always been for mothers of daughters; it's the wanting to protect your child that makes the mother end up wielding the big stick. What a hard time mothers have of it, at times it seems no way you can win.

Dear Mum, I don't think I'm expressing myself as well as I want to . . . you have had a very hard life, and your lessons have often been bitter; in turn you tried to hold me back when I went soaring for the clouds, I know now because you didn't want to see me hurt. It was wanting to go for the clouds that also made me need to break away and now as I come back, I want you to know how much I am aware of all I owe you, though at times I didn't realise it, or show gratitude. So many of the fighting qualities I imagined I personally invented came in fact from you; all your loving, and your strength, have been with me always, even the times I didn't know it. The rebel in me is in fact the rebel in you . . . it was only your sadness and tiredness quenched it; but it comes to life again, I hope, a little through me . . . I was so proud of you the day you came on the abortion demo – we had both come such a long way from the silence of when I was seventeen – and proud of you taking those anti-fascist leaflets into work; I've told everyone about it, and they think you're great! Of course, there will be things we won't agree about, but you're right, in the end it's the same things we want, and that's the important thing.

What I'm also trying to say is that all the times I rallied and railed it was in fact because I desperately wanted your approval and acceptance, didn't want just to be the 'nutter leftie' . . . because my politics, and those of my friends, do in fact often put us beyond the pale; Dad's right, there are certain jobs I'll never now be allowed to have, there are risks we all take, and sometimes you feel desperate, up against the brick wall of something that is so much bigger than us.

It's the politics, which for me pervade all of life, that make me want to write . . . the desire to somehow be able to communicate and help to change . . . Did I ever tell you I want to sometime write a novel or play about you? There – fame and immortality!

There's a show on next week I particularly want you to see because there's an actress in it that I'd like to play you when and if I finally get around to writing that play . . . she's bloody marvellous, and has a beautiful sympathetic touch, lots of strength, and a quite similar, cocky sense of humour.

And now I want to write out something for you that I meant to send a long time ago, but don't think I ever did. I heard it last year, after seeing a play about mothers and daughters. It was a feminist play, and tried to show how mothers oppress their daughters, precisely because they themselves are so oppressed; and how in turn daughters oppress their mothers, themselves take them for granted the way society does . . . then those daughters too become mothers and the vicious circle continues . . . except, the play said, if we join together and fight the forces that have divided us, then mothers will cease to try to bring up their little girls as Well-Behaved Young Women, and daughters cease to hypocritically want their mothers to be Model-Slave-Like Mums . . . and just love each other instead. It was a very moving play, and made me think and feel a lot, and how, for all I could rant on about MY wanting to be liberated, I still hadn't properly understood YOUR oppression, part of me still colluding with you-know-who about how dreadful it was that you weren't constantly up to your neck in Omosuds, Angel Delight and what- ever else it is that Super-Mums are supposed to chain themselves to . . .

> Even some revolutionaries are lovers,
>   even some poets have babies . . .
> I keep on wanting everything,
>   and I want you to want that too.

Words from the play: poetry and motion sung/ danced by women strong in their fragility, proud in their vulnerability as mothers, as daughters . . . let me stand up and be counted, every shiver, every shout! A beauty I was glad for, bringing tears in recognition; Mum I love you, Mum I'm glad I got away from you, Mum I *love* you and I wish you would come too.

Not anger, but sadness that I ever had to get away from you. What anger I have is reserved for those who taught you to be fatalistic, for those who encouraged us both to take taking you for granted, for granted.

And I remember my wanting to send you a copy of Gorky's *Childhood*, hoping that you would recognise yourself in the Great Mother; beautiful love, massive protector, my ever-smiling laughter learner. Just as I thank these women for daring their play, I thank Gorky for his mother; she brought me in touch with my love for you.

Like him, I too have had to fight from the worst lesson you ever taught me: the need to submit, a sad-eyed acceptance of 'this is how the world is'. Mother, my world must be how I make it . . . little as I knew it then, or you, my suicides were in fact my *love* for life; my wanting, oh, so much more than we as women were supposed to want . . . the journey through the stomach pumps taking me to where? . . . to here: standing now waving the manacles I have hacked away, delighted in my terrifying freedom –

And I remember now, too, all the good you ever taught me. For it was from you I learned to laugh, to joy, to give myself up to experience; no person has ever taught me as you have, to so grasp life. You showed me with your drunken tears, with your sad forties songs, with your compassion, your girlish jokes and, yes too, with your hate. Short on book learning, deep in emotion, it's you who've kept me from falling in for too long with the intellectuals, those dried up pedants who imagine that to think is the same as to feel; the gut-gripping life-destroying bloodily glorious REAL thing . . .

But you, Mum, you're ready and you're real. Your one fault was in teaching me to reach out only to surrender; but I've reached out and refused to surrender. I'm glad you taught me to reach out, and I'm glad I've learnt not to let go; and some day I pray you will joy in my victory – yet so strange to you – and be proud of your part in making me a lady hungry for victories. Little as you now accept it, the most loyal I could ever be by you is to finish the tales you were not allowed to write, to do honour to the visions you gave me, by straining for their reality . . .

You know you wouldn't really have wanted a *Woman's Own* Happy Ending for me. I'm different. Mum, the 'odd one out' in our family: at times I've been the mad man, the betrayer and the freak. But, in reality, my 'differentness' is only my giving credence to the dreams you first lent me . . . this idealism against which you warn me, it's yours too you know.

– Mine won't be an easy ride, mother, not ever, I don't think. Daily I pay the price for my 'differentness', for my refusal to conform. And there are times when I long to be anything other than what I am; to be able to be happily blind, to not see the suffering, to become one of those pink-varnished girls who stare adoringly up at their jail-keeper husband: blind, and partly dead, but accepted, oh accepted, *normal*.

But I have come too far, can never turn back now – and most times I am glad for that. I try, I fail, I sometimes even succeed; and I joy in my courage, even finding strength from that loneliness which has again and again become mine for my refusal to play the game. Because what I will not surrender is the free me, the one who is real, solid, blood, lust and all . . .

> I want
> what I guess, I have always wanted;
> – I keep on wanting everything,
> and I want you to want that too.

Mum, if only you knew it, that's your song I'm singing: it's you who taught me the tune, and it's for you I'll carry on singing it – and for my daughters' daughters; through the age-old strength of women, one day our day will come . . .

You'd better not show this letter to Dad – hide it somewhere, he'd throw a bloody blue fit . . .

Nuff for now. Write soon, let me know when to expect you, wear a black leather carnation so I'll recognise yer.

> Much and much and lots of lots and love too
> 'normous piles of it
> your one and only loving
> Personal Genius,
> Kate

From *Between Ourselves: Letters Between Mothers and Daughters 1750–1982*, edited by Karen Payne, published by Michael Joseph/Virago Press.

AUDRE LORDE,
'HOW I BECAME A POET'

'Wherever the bird with no feet flew she found trees with no limbs.'

When the strongest words for what I have to offer come out of me sounding like words I remember from my mother's mouth, then I either have to reassess the meaning of everything I have to say now, or re-examine the worth of her old words.

My mother had a special and secret relationship with words, taken for granted as language because it was always there. I did not speak until I was four. When I was three, the dazzling world of strange lights and fascinating shapes which I inhabited resolved itself in mundane definitions, and I learned another nature of things as seen through eyeglasses. This perception of things was less colourful and confusing but much more comfortable than the one native to my near-sighted and unevenly focused eyes.

I remember trundling along Lenox Avenue with my mother, on our way to school to pick up Phyllis and Helen for lunch. It was late spring because my legs felt light and real, unencumbered by bulky snow-pants. I dawdled along the fence around the public playground, inside of which grew one stunted plane tree. Enthralled, I stared up at the sudden revelation of each single and particular leaf of green, precisely shaped and laced about with unmixed light. Before my glasses, I had known trees as tall brown pillars ending in fat puffy swirls of paling greens, much like the pictures of them I perused in my sisters' story-books from which I learned so much of my visual world.

But out of my mother's mouth a world of comment came cascading when she felt at ease or in her element, full of picaresque constructions and surreal scenes.

We were never dressed too lightly, but rather 'in next kin to nothing'. *Neck skin to nothing?* Impassable and impossible distances were measured by the distance 'from Hog to Kick 'em Jenny'. *Hog? Kick 'em Jenny?* Who knew until I was sane and grown a poet with a mouthful of stars, that these were two little reefs in the Grenadines, between Grenada and Carriacou.

The euphemisms of body were equally puzzling, if no less colourful. A mild reprimand was accompanied not by a slap on the behind, but a 'smack on the backass', or on the 'bamsy'. You sat on your 'bam-bam', but anything between your hip-bones and upper thighs was consigned to the 'lower-region', a word I always imagined to have French origins, as in 'Don't forget to wash your *l'oregión* before you go to bed'. For more clinical and precise descriptions, there was always 'between your legs' – whispered.

The sensual content of life was masked and cryptic, but attended in well-coded phrases. Somehow all the cousins knew that Uncle Cyril couldn't lift heavy things because of his 'bam-bam-coo', and the lowered voice in which this hernia was spoken of warned us that it had something to do with 'down there'. And on the infrequent but magical occasions when mother performed her delicious laying on of hands for a crick in the neck or a pulled muscle, she didn't massage your backbone, she 'raised your zandalee'.

I never caught cold, but 'got co-hum, co-hum', and then everything turned 'cro-bo-so', topsy-turvy, or at least, a bit askew.

I am a reflection of my mother's secret poetry as well as of her hidden angers.

Sitting between my mother's spread legs, her strong knees gripping my shoulders tightly like some well-attended drum, my head in her lap, while she brushed and combed and oiled and braided. I feel my mother's strong, rough hands all up in my unruly hair, while I'm squirming around on a low stool or on a folded towel on the floor, my rebellious shoulders hunched and jerking against the inexorable sharp-toothed comb. After each springy portion is combed and braided, she pats it tenderly and proceeds to the next.

I hear the interjection of *sotto voce* admonitions that punctuated whatever discussion she and my father were having.

'Hold your back up, now! Deenie, keep still! Put your head so!' Scratch, scratch. 'When last you wash your hair? Look the dandruff!' Scratch, scratch, the comb's truth setting my own teeth on edge. Yet, these were some of the moments I missed most sorely when our real wars began.

I remember the warm mother smell caught between her legs, and the intimacy of our physical touching nestled inside of the anxiety/pain like a nutmeg nestled inside its covering of mace.

The radio, the scratching comb, the smell of petroleum jelly, the grip of her knees and my stinging scalp all fall into — *the rhythms of a litany, the rituals of Black women combing their daughter's hair.*

Saturday morning. The one morning of the week my mother does not leap from bed to prepare me and my sisters for school or church. I wake in the cot in their bedroom, knowing only it is one of those lucky days when she is still in bed, and alone. My father is in the kitchen. The sound of pots and the slightly off-smell of frying bacon mixes with the smell of percolating Bokar coffee.

The click of her wedding ring against the wooden headboard. She is awake. I get up and go over and crawl into my mother's bed. Her smile. Her glycerine-flannel smell. The warmth. She reclines upon her back and side, one arm extended, the other flung across her forehead. A hot-water bottle wrapped in body-temperature flannel, which she used to quiet her gall-bladder pains during the night. Her large soft breasts beneath the buttoned flannel of her nightgown. Below, the rounded swell of her stomach, silent and inviting touch.

I crawl against her, playing with the enflannelled, warm, rubber bag, pummelling it, tossing it, sliding it down the roundness of her stomach to the warm sheet between the bend of her elbow and the curve of her waist below her breasts, flopping sideward inside the printed cloth. Under the covers, the morning smells soft and sunny and full of promise.

I frolic with the liquid-filled water bottle, patting and rubbing its firm giving softness. I shake it slowly, rocking it back and forth, lost in sudden tenderness, at the same time gently rubbing against my mother's quiet body. Warm milky smells of morning surround us.

Feeling the smooth deep firmness of her breasts against my shoulders, my pajama'd back, sometimes, more daringly, against my ears and the sides of my cheeks. Tossing, tumbling, the soft gurgle of the water within its rubber casing. Sometimes the thin sound of her ring against the bedstead as she moves her hand up over my head. Her arm comes down across me, holding me to her for a moment, then quiets my frisking.

'All right, now.'

I nuzzle against her sweetness, pretending not to hear.

'All right, now, I said; stop it. It's time to get up from this bed. Look lively, and mind you spill that water.'

Before I can say anything she is gone in a great deliberate heave. The purposeful whip of her chenille robe over her warm flannel gown and the bed already growing cold beside me.

'Wherever the bird with no feet flew she found trees with no limbs.'

* * *

When I was growing up in my mother's house, there were spices you grated and spices you pounded, and whenever you pounded spice and garlic or other herbs, you used a mortar. Every West Indian woman worth her salt had her own mortar. Now if you lost or broke your mortar, you could, of course, buy another one in the market over on Park Avenue, under the bridge, but those were usually Puerto Rican mortars, and even though they were made out of wood and worked exactly the same way, somehow they were never really as good as West Indian mortars. Now where the best mortars came from I was never really sure, but I knew it must be in the vicinity of that amorphous and mystically perfect place called 'home'. And whatever came from 'home' was bound to be special.

My mother's mortar was an elaborate affair, quite at variance with most of her other possessions, and certainly with her projected public view of herself. It stood, solid and elegant, on a shelf in the kitchen cabinet for as long as I can remember, and I loved it dearly.

The mortar was of a foreign fragrant wood, too dark for cherry and too red for walnut. To my child eyes, the outside was carved in an intricate and most enticing manner. There were rounded plums and oval indeterminate fruit, some long and fluted like a banana, others ovular and end-swollen like a ripe alligator pear. In between these were smaller rounded shapes like cherries, lying in batches against and around each other.

I loved to finger the hard roundness of the carved fruit, and the always surprising termination of the shapes as the carvings stopped at the rim and the bowl sloped abruptly downward, smoothly oval but suddenly businesslike. The heavy sturdiness of this useful wooden object always made me feel secure and somehow full; as if it conjured up from all the many different flavours pounded into the inside wall, visions of delicious feasts both once enjoyed and still to come.

The pestle was long and tapering, fashioned from the same mysterious rose-deep wood, and fitted into the hand almost casually, familiarly. The actual shape reminded me of a summer crook-necked squash uncurled and slightly twisted. It could have been an avocado, with the neck of the alligator pear elongated and the whole made efficient for pounding, without ever losing the apparent soft firmness and the character of the fruit which the wood suggested. It was slightly bigger at the grinding end than most pestles, and the widened curved end fitted into the bowl of the mortar easily. Long use and years of impact and grinding within the bowl's worn hollow had softened the very surface of the wooden pestle, until a thin layer of split fibres coated the rounded end like a layer of velvet. A layer of the same velvety mashed wood lined the bottom inside the sloping bowl.

My mother did not particularly like to pound spice, and she looked upon the advent of powdered everything as a cook's boon. But there were some certain dishes that called for a particular savoury blending of garlic, raw onion and pepper, and souse was one of them.

For our mother's souse, it didn't matter what kind of meat was used. You could have hearts, or beefends, or even chicken backs and gizzards when we were really poor. It was the pounded-up saucy blend of herb and spice rubbed into the meat before it was left to stand so for a few hours before cooking that made that dish so special and unforgettable. But my mother had some very firm ideas about what she liked best to cook and about which were her favourite dishes, and souse was definitely not one of either.

On the very infrequent occasions that my mother would allow one of us three girls to choose a meal – as opposed to helping to prepare it, which was a daily routine – on those occasions my sisters would usually choose one of those proscribed dishes so dear to our hearts remembered from our relatives' tables, contraband, and so very rare in our house. They might ask for hot dogs, perhaps, smothered in ketchup sauce, or with crusty Boston-baked beans; or American chicken, breaded first and fried crispy the way the southern people did it; or creamed something-or-other that one of my sisters had tasted at school; what-have-you croquettes or anything fritters; or once even a daring outrageous request for slices of fresh watermelon, hawked from the back of a rickety wooden pickup truck with the southern road-dust still on her slatted sides, from which a young bony Black man with a turned-around baseball cap on his head would hang and half-yell, half-yodel – 'Wahr – deeeeeee – mayyyyyyy-lawnnnnnnn'.

There were many American dishes I longed for too, but on the one or two occasions a year that I got to choose a meal, I would always ask for souse. That way, I knew that I would get to use my mother's mortar, and this in itself was more treat for me than any of the forbidden foods. Besides, if I really wanted hot dogs or anything croquettes badly enough, I could steal some money from my father's pocket and buy them in the school lunch.

'Mother, let's have souse,' I'd say, and never even stop to think about it. The anticipated taste of the soft spicy meat had become inseparable in my mind from the tactile pleasures of using my mother's mortar.

'But what makes you think anybody can find time to mash up all that stuff?' My mother would cut her hawk-grey eyes at me from beneath their heavy black brows. 'Among-you children never stop to think,' and she'd turn back to whatever it was she had been doing. If she had just come from the office with my father, she might be checking the day's receipts, or she might be washing the endless piles of dirty linen that always seemed to issue from rooming-houses.

'Oh, I'll pound the garlic, Mommy!' would be my next line in the script written by some ancient and secret hand, and off I'd go to the cabinet to get down the heavy wooden mortar and pestle.

I took a head of garlic out from the garlic bottle in the icebox, and breaking off ten or twelve cloves from the head, I carefully peeled away the tissue lavender skin, slicing each stripped peg in half lengthwise. I dropped them piece by piece into the capacious waiting bowl of the mortar. Taking a slice from a small onion, I put the rest aside to be used later over the meat, and cutting the slice into quarters, I tossed it into the mortar also. Next came the coarsely ground fresh black pepper, and then a lavish blanketing cover of salt over the whole. Last, if we had any, a few leaves from the top of a head of celery. My mother sometimes added a slice of green pepper, but I did not like the texture of the pepper-skin under the pestle, and preferred to add it along with the sliced onion later on, leaving it all to sit over the seasoned and resting meat.

After all the ingredients were in the bowl of the mortar, I fetched the pestle and placing it into the bowl, slowly rotated the shaft a few times, working it gently down through all the ingredients to mix them. Only then would I lift the pestle, and with one hand firmly pressed around the carved side of the mortar caressing the wooden fruit with my aromatic fingers, I thrust sharply downward, feeling the shifting salt and the hard little pellets of garlic right up through the shaft of the wooden pestle. Up again, down, around, and up – so the rhythm began.

To *thud push rub rotate up* repeated over and over. The muted thump of the pestle on the bed of grinding spice as the salt and pepper absorbed the slowly yielding juices of the garlic and celery leaves.

Thud push rub rotate up. The mingling fragrances rising from the bowl of the mortar.

Thud push rub rotate up. The feeling of the pestle held between my curving fingers, and the mortar's outside rounding like fruit into my palm as I steadied it against my body.

All these transported me into a world of scent and rhythm and movement and sound that grew more and more exciting as the ingredients liquefied.

Sometimes my mother would look over at me with that amused annoyance which passed for tenderness.

'What you think you making there, garlic soup? Enough, go get the meat now.' And I would fetch the lamb hearts, for instance, from the icebox and begin to prepare them. Cutting away the hardened veins at the top of the smooth firm muscles, I divided each oval heart into four wedge-shaped pieces, and taking a bit of the spicy mash from the mortar with my fingertips, I rubbed each piece with the savoury mix, the pungent smell of garlic and onion and celery enveloping the kitchen.

The last day I ever pounded seasoning for souse was in the summer of my fifteenth year. It had been a fairly unpleasant summer for me. I had just finished my first year in high school. Instead of being able to visit my newly found friends, all of whom lived in other parts of the city, I had had to accompany my mother on a round of doctors with whom she would have long whispered conversations. Only a matter of utmost importance could have kept her away from the office for so many mornings in a row. But my mother was concerned because I was fourteen and a half years old and had not yet menstruated, I had breasts but no period, and she was afraid there was something 'wrong' with me. Yet, since she had never discussed this mysterious business of menstruation with me, I was certainly not supposed to know what all this whispering was about, even though it concerned my own body.

Of course, I knew as much as I could have possibly found out in those days from the hard-to-get books on the 'closed shelf' behind the librarian's desk at the public library, where I had brought a forged note from home in order to be allowed to read them, sitting under the watchful eye of the librarian at a special desk reserved for that purpose.

Although not terribly informative, they were fascinating books, and used words like *menses* and *ovulation* and *vagina*.

But four years before, I had had to find out if I

was going to become pregnant, because a boy from school much bigger than me had invited me up to the roof on my way home from the library and then threatened to break my glasses if I didn't let him stick his 'thing' between my legs. And at that time I knew only that being pregnant had something to do with sex, and sex had something to do with that thin pencil-like 'thing' and was in general nasty and not to be talked about by nice people, and I was afraid my mother might find out and what would she do to me then? I was not supposed to be looking at the mailboxes in the hallway of that house anyway, even though Doris was a girl in my class at St Mark's who lived in that house and I was always so lonely in the summer, particularly that summer when I was ten.

So after I got home I washed myself up and lied about why I was late getting home from the library and got a whipping for being late. That must have been a hard summer for my parents at the office too, because that was the summer that I got a whipping for something or other almost every day between the Fourth of July and Labour Day.

When I wasn't getting whippings, I hid out at the library on 135th Street, and forged notes from my mother to get books from the 'closed shelf', and read about sex and having babies, and waited to become pregnant. None of the books were very clear to me about the relationship between having your period and having a baby, but they were all very clear about the relationship between penises and getting pregnant. Or maybe the confusion was all in my own mind, because I had always been a very fast but not a very careful reader.

So four years later, in my fifteenth year, I was a

very scared little girl, still half-afraid that one of that endless stream of doctors would look up into my body and discover my four-year-old shame and say to my mother, 'Aha! So that's what's wrong! Your daughter is about to become pregnant!'

On the other hand, if I let Mother know that I knew what was happening and what these medical safaris were all about, I would have to answer her questions about how and wherefore I knew, since she hadn't told me, divulging in the process the whole horrible and self-incriminating story of forbidden books and forged library notes and rooftops and stairwell conversations.

It was a year after the rooftop incident, when we had moved farther uptown. The kids at St Catherine's seemed to know a lot more about sex than at St Mark's. In the eighth grade, I had stolen money and bought my classmate Adeline a pack of cigarettes and she had confirmed my bookish suspicions about how babies were made. My response to her graphic descriptions had been to think to myself, *there obviously must be another way that Adeline doesn't know about, because my parents have children and I know they never did anything like that!* But the basic principles were all there, and sure enough they were the same as I had gathered from *The Young People's Family Book*.

So in my fifteenth summer, on examining table after examining table, I kept my legs open and my mouth shut, and when I saw blood on my pants one hot July afternoon, I rinsed them out secretly in the bathroom and put them back on wet because I didn't know how to break the news to my mother that both her worries and mine were finally over. (All this time

I had at least understood that having your period was a sign you were not pregnant.)

What then happened felt like a piece of an old and elaborate dance between my mother and me. She discovers finally, through a stain on the toilet seat left there on purpose by me as a mute announcement, what has taken place; she scolds, 'Why didn't you tell me about all of this, now? It's nothing to get upset over, you are a woman, not a child any more. Now you go over to the drugstore and ask the man for . . .'

I was just relieved the whole damn thing was over with. It's difficult to talk about double messages without having a twin tongue. Nightmarish evocations and restrictions were being verbalised by my mother:

'This means from now on you better watch your step and not be so friendly with every Tom, Dick, and Harry . . .' (which must have meant my staying late after school to talk with my girlfriends, because I did not even know any boys); and, 'Now remember, too, after you wrap up your soiled napkins in newspaper, don't leave them hanging around on the bathroom floor where you father has to see them, not that it's anything shameful but all the same, remember . . .'

Along with all of these admonitions, there was something else coming from my mother that I could not define. It was the lurking of that amused/annoyed brow-furrowed half-smile of hers that made me feel – all her nagging words to the contrary – that something very good and satisfactory and pleasing to her had just happened, and that we were both pretending otherwise for some very wise and secret reasons. I would come to understand these reasons later, as a reward, if I handled myself properly. Then, at the end of it all, my mother thrust the box of Kotex at me

(I had fetched it in its plain wrapper back from the drugstore, along with a sanitary belt), saying to me, 'But look now what time it is already, I wonder what we're going to eat for supper tonight?' She waited. At first I didn't understand, but I quickly picked up the cue. I had seen the beefends in the icebox that morning.

'Mommy, please let's have some souse – I'll pound the garlic.' I dropped the box on to a kitchen chair and started to wash my hands in anticipation.

'Well, go put your business away first. What did I tell you about leaving that lying around?' She wiped her hands from the washtub where she had been working and handed the plain wrapped box of Kotex back to me.

'I have to go out, I forgot to pick up tea at the store. Now make sure you rub the meat good.'

When I came back into the kitchen, my mother had left. I moved toward the kitchen cabinet to fetch down the mortar and pestle. My body felt new and special and unfamiliar and suspect all at the same time.

I could feel bands of tension sweeping across my body back and forth, like lunar winds across the moon's face. I felt the slight rubbing bulge of the cotton pad between my legs, and I smelled the delicate breadfruit smell rising up from the front of my print blouse that was my own woman smell, warm, shameful, but secretly utterly delicious.

Years afterward when I was grown, whenever I thought about the way I smelled that day, I would have a fantasy of my mother, her hands wiped dry from the washing, and her apron untied and laid neatly away, looking down upon me lying on the couch, and then slowly, thoroughly, our touching and caressing each other's most secret places.

I took the mortar down, and smashed the cloves of garlic with the edge of its underside, to loosen the thin papery skins in a hurry. I sliced them and flung them into the mortar's bowl along with some black pepper and celery leaves. The white salt poured in, covering the garlic and black pepper and pale chartreuse celery fronds like a snowfall. I tossed in the onion and some bits of green pepper and reached for the pestle.

It slipped through my fingers and clattered to the floor, rolling around in a semicircle back and forth, until I bent to retrieve it. I grabbed the head of the wooden stick and straightened up, my ears ringing faintly. Without even wiping it, I plunged the pestle into the bowl, feeling the blanket of salt give way, and the broken cloves of garlic just beneath. The downward thrust of the wooden pestle slowed upon contact, rotated back and forth slowly, and then gently altered its rhythm to include an up and down beat. Back and forth, round, up and down, back, forth, round, round, up and down . . . There was a heavy fullness at the root of me that was exciting and dangerous.

As I continued to pound the spice, a vital connection seemed to establish itself between the muscles of my fingers curved tightly around the smooth pestle in its insistent downward motion, and the molten core of my body whose source emanated from a new ripe fullness just beneath the pit of my stomach. That invisible thread, taut and sensitive as a clitoris exposed, stretched through my curled fingers up my round brown arm into the moist reality of my armpits, whose warm sharp odour with a strange new overlay mixed with the ripe garlic smells from the mortar and the general sweat-heavy aromas of high summer.

The thread ran over my ribs and along my spine, tingling and singing, into a basin that was poised between my hips, now pressed against the low kitchen counter before which I stood, pounding spice. And within that basin was a tiding ocean of blood beginning to be made real and available to me for strength and information.

The jarring shocks of the velvet-lined pestle, striking the bed of spice, travelled up an invisible pathway along the thread into the centre of me, and the harshness of the repeated impacts became increasingly more unbearable. The tidal basin suspended between my hips shuddered at each repetition of the strokes which now felt like assaults. Without my volition my downward thrusts of the pestle grew gentler and gentler, until its velvety surface seemed almost to caress the liquefying mash at the bottom of the mortar.

The whole rhythm of my movements softened and elongated, until, dreamlike, I stood, one hand tightly curved around the carved mortar, steadying it against the middle of my body; while my other hand, around the pestle, rubbed and pressed the moistening spice into readiness with a sweeping circular movement.

I hummed tunelessly to myself as I worked in the warm kitchen, thinking with relief about how simple my life would be now that I had become a woman. The catalogue of dire menstruation-warnings from my mother passed out of my head. My body felt strong and full and open, yet captivated by the gentle motions of the pestle, and the rich smells filling the kitchen, and the fullness of the young summer heat.

I heard my mother's key in the lock.

She swept into the kitchen briskly, like a ship under full sail. There were tiny beads of sweat over her upper lip, and vertical creases between her brows.

'You mean to tell me no meat is ready?' My mother dropped her parcel of tea on to the table, and looking over my shoulder, sucked her teeth loudly in weary disgust. 'What do you call yourself doing, now? You have all night to stand up there playing with the food? I go all the way to the store and back already and still you can't mash up a few pieces of garlic to season some meat? But you know how to do the thing better than this! Why you vex me so?'

She took the mortar and pestle out of my hands and started to grind vigorously. And there were still bits of garlic left at the bottom of the bowl.

'Now you do, so!' She brought the pestle down inside the bowl of the mortar with dispatch, crushing the last of the garlic. I heard the thump of wood brought down heavily upon wood, and I felt the harsh impact throughout my body, as if something had broken inside of me. Thump, thump, went the pestle, purposefully, up and down in the old familiar way.

'It was getting mashed, Mother,' I dared to protest, turning away to the icebox. 'I'll fetch the meat.' I was surprised at my own brazenness in answering back.

But something in my voice interrupted my mother's efficient motions. She ignored my implied contradiction, itself an act of rebellion strictly forbidden in our house. The thumping stopped.

'What's wrong with you, now? Are you sick? You want to go to your bed?'

'No, I'm all right, Mother.'

But I felt her strong fingers on my upper arm, turning me around, her other hand under my chin as she peered into my face. Her voice softened.

'Is it your period making you so slow-down today?' She gave my chin a little shake, as I looked up into her hooded grey eyes, now becoming almost gentle. The kitchen felt suddenly oppressively hot and still, and I felt myself beginning to shake all over.

Tears I did not understand started from my eyes, as I realised that my old enjoyment of the bone-jarring way I had been taught to pound spice would feel different to me from now on, and also that in my mother's kitchen there was only one right way to do anything. Perhaps my life had not become so simple, after all.

My mother stepped away from the counter and put her heavy arm around my shoulders. I could smell the warm herness rising from between her arm and her body, mixed with the smell of glycerine and rosewater, and the scent of her thick bun of hair.

'I'll finish up the food for supper.' She smiled at me, and there was a tenderness in her voice and an absence of annoyance that was welcome, although unfamiliar.

'You come inside now and lie down on the couch and I'll make you a hot cup of tea.'

Her arm across my shoulders was warm and slightly damp. I rested my head upon her shoulder, and realised with a shock of pleasure and surprise that I

was almost as tall as my mother, as she led me into
the cool darkened parlour.

From *Zami: A New Spelling of my Name*, published by
Sheba Feminist Publishers.

MARILYN FRENCH
from
HER MOTHER'S DAUGHTER

My mother lived to be old, although she always said she would die young. All through my childhood she warned me – threatened me? – that because of her defective heart, she would depart early from this vale of tears, whereas my sturdy peasantlike father would live forever, drowning the memory of her fastidiously prepared meals in canned pork and beans, which he would enjoy just as much. When I was fifteen and searching through her bureau drawers one afternoon – hoping, probably, to discover some clue as to how she felt about me – I found a sealed envelope marked 'To Be Opened After My Death'. In a rage I tore it open, pulled out a piece of stationery, and found that her Limoges china service for eight (with some missing), her five crystal water goblets (one had broken), and her silver service for eight were to be evenly divided between my sister and me. Still furi-

ous, I burned the thing, and as it went up, I panicked
and threw it into the toilet. The paper kept burning,
so I slammed down the lid, not realising it was plastic
and flammable. When the toilet seat began to burn,
I called the fire department. The neighbours clucked
their tongues for weeks afterward about young girls
sneaking cigarettes when their mothers were away
from home. My mother not only didn't get angry,
but she invited me to sit in the backyard with her
and smoke. She never wrote another will. I checked.

In any case, her flawed heart did not noticeably
shorten her life. She lived long, only she shrank. Or
maybe my body blew up over the years, so that when
we appeared together in the full-length mirror in the
bridal shop dressing room where we were trying on
dresses for my daughter's wedding, we looked like
creatures from two different species. I can remember
when we looked alike, when strangers recognised us
as mother and daughter. But now she is tiny and frail
for all her middle bulk. Her bones, her very skull,
are delicate, smaller than a child's, and the flesh has
shrivelled on her arms and knit itself so tight on
her small face that her eyes have almost disappeared.
Whereas I am tall and broad-shouldered and thick (I
don't quite know when that happened) and my face
shines like a swollen moon. It wasn't even that we
looked like two versions of the same product, one
designed for light home use and the other for heavy
industry; we looked like two different kinds of creature, like a fat smooth rhino and a wrinkled impala.
If you knew that we were mother and daughter,
you would suspect some mysterious voodoo process
whereby I grew by sucking in all her fluids. Like
midges. Midge mothers do not lay eggs, they repro-

duce young from inside their bodies without benefit of clergy, state, or even any informal male assistance. And the baby develops inside the mother's body, not in a uterus, but in her tissues, and eventually, she fills her whole body, as she devours it from the inside. When she is ready to be born, she breaks out of her mother/prison, leaving behind only a chitinous shell. They never have mother-daughter squabbles: midge mothers may sacrifice themselves entirely for their young, but the young never have to hear about it. It is also true, of course, that young so produced begin within two days to reproduce themselves in the same way. They hardly have time to complain about the quality of their lives.

Women of the past had no time for that either, and my mother has little sympathy for those who complain about the quality of life, feeling, I suspect, somewhat like a midge mother. Still, as she stood there in the dressing room mirror, miserable at the poor fit of the dresses she was trying on, wanting to look splendid for Arden's wedding, she swung her head away from the mirror angrily. I looked down on that tiny head and I wanted to caress it, to console her as one does a child, by touching, affection. But my mother is not a woman to be consoled. Her head is stiff on her neck. She gazed in the mirror again, not seeing that her lined faced was unblemished by age spots or that her fine soft hair was still blond, and made a foul face at that person in the mirror, and asked me if that was really how she looked.

When my mother was in her heyday – her second heyday, but the only one I saw – that is, when my sister and I were grown and married and she had a little money and leisure, she had her hair cut in a

soft short bob called a feather cut, and went to an
expensive shop and bought beautiful clothes. I still
remember them: she had a red wool suit with a short
jacket collared in leopard, and a black wool suit with
a high round neck trimmed with mink, a navy blue
wool dress with a skirt cut on the bias so it whirled
when she walked, and a short white wool knit jacket,
double-breasted with gold buttons. She drove an old
Cadillac, and announced her address proudly to sales-
women in the good shops. Into these shops she carried a stiff smile, eyebrows that seemed permanently
raised, and her fine clothes. These shops were the
only place she could obtain the sense of having a
public life. Sometimes she and my father went out
to dinner, but in those years she was so loudly disap-
proving of restaurant food that my embarrassed father
resisted going. They played bridge once a week with
my aunt and uncle, but a formal suit was a bit too
warm for such an occasion. She seemed relatively
content in those years.

But when she aged, her body changed. She grew
shorter, the skin on her arms and legs shrivelled, and
she expanded in the middle. Her middle got to be
four sizes bigger than the rest of her. It was impossible
to find fine clothes to fit this alien body, and she
began to buy polyester pantsuits with expandable
waistbands, or wraparound skirts. One day, during a
winter when she and my father were visiting Palm
Beach, they walked into a shop on Worth Avenue,
and the owner blocked their passage, asking rudely
what they wanted. 'A golf jacket,' my mother blurted
angrily. He nodded his head brusquely to the left.
'Try down the block. We don't have them.' She never
got over this incident. 'He wouldn't even let us in,

Anastasia! How did he know we wouldn't buy anything? What was it, do you think? Was it because
we're old? Because my clothes look cheap?' She told
this story repeatedly, always ending it with the same
questions: she must have forgotten she had asked
them before. I was never able to find answers that
satisfied her.

It tormented her so that she was still talking about
it a decade later, and I got the sense that the incident
had plunged into a recurrent nightmare. As if you
suddenly found yourself in real life peeing in a toilet
exposed to a room full of people, or saw your hair
falling out in clumps, or whatever your recurrent
nightmare is. The storekeeper had treated her with
contempt. It occurred to me that she had arranged
her life so that she would never be exposed to contempt. Certainly none of her family would think of
treating her contemptuously. Her husband treats her
like his sovereign; sometimes he even refers to her as
'my lady'. And my sister and I and our children also
defer to her as if she were royalty. We placate her,
fuss over her, wait on her. When we speak, we direct
our faces toward her and enunciate very distinctly, so
she can read our lips as we speak. When we cook
for her, we avoid oil, onions, garlic, most spices. She
is helped, by someone, in and out of cars, up and
down stairs, and even through doorways, because she
is feeble, arthritic, and subject to the dizziness caused
by inner-car disease. My daughter's husband, meeting
her for the first time, found her a grande dame. I
was surprised to hear him say that. I had never seen
my mother that way.

Not at all. We didn't defer because we feared her,
because she held power that could strip us of our

estates or rank, or heap them on us if we pleased her. We did it because . . . we always had. Because Daddy did. Because she seemed to need us to do it. It didn't seem much to give her, making her the centre, deferring. Because somehow we understood that she had suffered more than anyone, more than any of us, and that in some sense we were responsible for her suffering. When I was a child I could not understand in what way it was my fault that Jesus had died, or how it was he died for me. I felt rather indignant about the whole thing: *I* certainly hadn't wanted him to die, and I failed to see how his doing so had in any way helped me. But I had no trouble whatever understanding that my mother had in some sense died for me, that she was a kind of midge mother whose effort had been so extraordinary that she had saved us, my sister and me, from being midge mothers in our turn. Because we are not midge mothers, we had vitality and pleasure and strength even after we had children. So we laid it at her feet, our vitality and strength, and tried to give her pleasure too. That was difficult though, and became increasingly so as she aged. She would watch our gyrations, our efforts to serve and please, like a bored dying aristocrat who knows that her servants are well-paid to please her. There was a cold distance in her eye, and sometimes a sneer of contempt upon her lips or a mocking edge in her voice. Visitors would see my father offer her tea and shawls, me offer Scotch and sympathy, my sister, with an edge of hysteria in her voice, trying to make her laugh by recounting a recent family mishap, and they would perceive a family pattern, and try to fit in, as was appropriate. I would watch her watching them, and I knew what she was thinking:

Nothing, nothing you do can console me for the loss of my life. I heard it, I saw it, I understood. For only I knew her heart.

I am talking about my mother in the past tense as if she were dead, but she isn't. Her walk is as tottering as an infant's and her breathing sounds like the cooing of pigeons; she is nearly blind and nearly deaf even with her hearing aid; and she is afraid to cross a street or climb a staircase because of her continual dizziness. But her mind is sharp and she looks marvellous and people praise her looks. She smiles like a knife edge, but they do not recognise that: she is an old lady, and all old ladies are sweet.

When we are alone, she grimaces and mocks them: 'Oh, the sweet old lady! That's what they think!' Then falls silent, sips her Scotch and holds the liquid in her mouth a long time before she swallows it. When she was still smoking, she'd light another forbidden delight. 'I don't *feel* old,' she'd protest. She'd sit up suddenly, as if energy had returned to her limbs and announce, 'I feel eighteen. Twelve!' Nine, I would think. You feel nine.

My mother feels nine; I feel older than she. She has not noticed that I have aged. She seems to expect me to look as I did at thirty, slim and untouched by lines or grey hair, and she gazes at my increased girth critically, and wonders why my hair is so dull. She doesn't realise that I have as many pairs of eyeglasses as she and that my hearing is not as good as it was. 'You always had wonderful hearing, Anastasia,' she says if I mention the subject. Better than hers, is what she means. And good legs. These were her two wishes for her first daughter, the spells she wrought to undo her own baleful influence – bad hearing and thick legs. I do not know if she thought she had any gift to offer me. I suspect not.

* * *

Last time I visited my mother, I came to feel very low as we sat around talking, and I told her about a fight I'd had with Arden. She'd been awful for a long time, hanging around the house smoking, glaring at me; playing the piano at its loudest, banging her way through every book of music in the house without bothering to correct the mistakes in any one piece; and refusing to help clean up, even to clean her own room. Not that the house ever really looks cleaned up even when it is, but with Arden around, it was beginning to look like a bus terminal. Then one night she opened the door to my developing closet even though the red light was signalling I was working inside and needed dark – something she's known since she was an infant. She wanted the car keys, and for some reason I'd taken my handbag inside with me. But I screamed. She'd completely ruined a dozen negatives I couldn't replace. I was a wild woman, I shouted, I yelled, I tore my own hair. She shrugged. 'I needed the car keys. I couldn't wait for hours until you came out.' She was sullen, surly, and I felt as if all the blood in my body had mounted to my head, and I slapped her, hard, across the mouth.

That was unusual enough, since I was never given to physical punishment, but she took it as a declaration of war. She slapped me back, I slapped her, we hauled into each other, twisting arms, socking each other, slapping. I was quickly reduced to pinching and twisting, because my daughter, although shorter and lighter than I, had studied karate, and had twenty-five years less smoking to slow her down. She got me pinned: I couldn't move: she shoved me backward, on to the arm of a stuffed chair.

'I could kill you now!' she hissed.

'Go ahead!' I yelled. 'It would be a blessed release from living with you!'

She let me go then, grabbed my bag and took the car keys, and stormed out of the apartment, slamming the door behind her.

This was the story I told my parents, and as I finished, my mother began to cry. I was astonished.

'Why are you crying?'

My father looked at me as if I were stupid. 'She feels bad for you, Ana. Of course she'd cry.'

Nonsense, I thought. She's never cried for me in her life. I turned to my mother, and asked again, severely, 'Why are you crying?'

She was sobbing now. 'Oh, I wish I could have talked to *my* mother like that! I never talked to her, I never told her how I felt, I never knew how she felt, and now it's too late!'

Well, that rocked me. Because in all the years I'd listened to my mother's tales, there had been these two, my mother and her mother, two throbbing figures in a landscape of concrete, suffering, separately yet linked, like wounded animals wandering through miles of silent tree trunks oblivious to their pain. Like a woman I saw once, walking down the street in Hempstead with a man on one side of her and a woman on the other, holding her arms. She was youngish – in her early thirties, and pretty, a little plump – but there was something on her face that made my heart tremble for her... No one else seemed to notice anything odd, people walked past her, around her, and did not glance twice at her. But that night I saw her picture in the newspaper: she was the only survivor of a fire that had killed her husband and her four children.

That was my image of them, these two women, Mommy and Grandma. And I had never had any inkling that anything lay in the space between them except their shared knowledge of grief. It was blind of me, of course, it simply makes sense that there had to be more. All my life I had rejected prettied pictures of life, slamming shut the saccharin children's books I was given at school, pulling wry faces in movie houses, questioning angrily people's sweetened explanations for things. I was an offensive child, and perhaps am an offensive adult, responding indignantly to anything that seems facile, designed to conceal, smooth over, sweeten, a reality I know to be grim and terrible. I would insult my mother's friends, announcing in outrage, 'I don't believe that!' or making faces at their gushing, swooping voices as they insisted that people were good and life was nice. Or the reverse.

Yet here I had all these years simply accepted as truth my mother's relation to her mother as one of total, unswerving love and devotion. Certainly, that was all I had ever heard or seen. My mother said her mother was a saint, and a saint was what I saw too. Quiet, sad, Grandma would sit in a small corner of the couch when she visited and open her arms to me, and I'd sit beside her and she'd take my hands in hers – so soft, as if the wrinkles had changed the texture of the fabric of her skin – and smile with

love, saying, 'My Anastasia, my little Anastasia'. She
and my mother would talk together in the kitchen
in Polish, and my grandmother would laugh and nod
her head. No anger ever came out of her voice or
showed on her face. I can't imagine her angry. She
would just cry when her grandson, my cousin, kicked
her when she tried to put him to bed. She never
raised her voice. Once, when she was visiting us, she
and my mother walked the two miles to the German
pork butcher for chops for dinner, and the butcher's
wife said something to her husband in German.
When they left the shop, my grandmother giggled:
she was pleased at being able to understand their
language without their knowing. What the woman
had said was 'What a gentle face that woman has!'
She was talking about my grandmother.

And whenever my mother spoke of her late at
night, her voice would grow foggy and her eyes
teary: 'My mother was a saint.' Then her voice would
thicken: 'Poor Momma.' And then she'd go off
towards one part of it, some part of it, the incredibly
cruel man, the submissive woman, the brutalised
children; or the poverty or the ignorance. All of it
hurt her, my mother, equally, although when she
came to the ignorance, her voice grew an edge, a
bitterness that sometimes seemed almost ready to spill
over on to her mother. But if I probed that, she
would shrug: 'What could she do? She knew
nothing.' When she spoke of the other things, she
spoke like a child: her voice was high and thin and
her sentences simple. And through it all, the same
shrug, the same sigh: 'I was such a stupid kid. I didn't
know anything.'

This is a part of my mother no one but me has

seen. I know her as the nine-year-old she had been
and in some way remains. My father would not want
to listen to such grief; he doesn't like problems unless
they are solvable mechanically, like a broken clock
or a stuck window. These he enjoys, and brings
considerable ingenuity to solving. Nor does my sister
enjoy harping on past sorrows. She likes to pull herself up and address the present, finding in present
action the only solution to past loss. And I am like
her in that – at least, I always used to be, or anyway,
I thought I was. Yet what have I been doing all these
years, sitting with mother in the dimly lighted room
as the clock hand moves silently toward four, smoke
clouding the air? (My father, who in the days when
he worked had to get up early in the morning, was
forced to go to bed by one at the latest, had gone
sighing and grumbling upstairs. At two or so, he
would get up noisily and go to the bathroom for a
heavy towel, which he would insert in the crack
between his bedroom door and the floor to keep the
odour of cigarette smoke from rising into his sleep –
his small protest and reproach to us.) My mother and
I agree to have just one more drink, and I get them,
although sometimes at that hour (this was long ago),
my mother would insist on getting up herself and
making our drinks. But I would always follow her
out to the kitchen while she did it, and carry my
own back to the little room she called the porch
where we would sit and talk. What have I been
doing, listening over and over, asking over and over,
obsessed with something, unsure what? Listening,
putting myself into her, becoming her, becoming my
grandmother, losing myself, as if I could once and
finally lose myself inside my mother, and in the pro-

cess give her the strength and hope she needs. Return the liquids I drained from her, become a midge mother in return, mothering my own mother.

And she would never tell these things to anyone else. Not even her sister, who 'doesn't know, she wasn't there, she didn't see what I saw, she doesn't remember, she thinks Poppa was wonderful, she doesn't want to hear anything else'. No, only I know this part of my mother, but it is her deepest part, the truest, the core. So when other people say things about her, I just look at them. I don't know what they are talking about.

And other people do say things about her. She is a difficult woman. She is deaf or nearly deaf, and angry about that: she gets irritated with people who speak softly, and grimaces and turns her head away disdainfully. People who don't understand what is happening think she is bored and rude. It is risky to give her a gift. She receives gifts, as well as certain acts designed to please, as challenges to which she is more than equal: she will in some way make sure the giver knows they have not managed to please her.

She is worst of all in restaurants, especially if one of us, my sister or I, have taken her. The place is invariably too noisy: with her hearing aid on, she cannot filter sounds, and the scrape of fork on plate, or chair on floor, are as importunate as the sound of voices on her receiver. Usually, the place is too cold as well. Beyond that, the food is never good. My sister strains her budget to take Mother to dinner for her birthday, and is – as always – gay and brittle over the clams casino, the mushroom soup, the medaillions de veau. 'Isn't this great?' she exhorts Mother. 'Isn't it delicious?' Mother's mouth twists into a stiff smile. 'Very good,' she obviously lies.

Later, to me, she almost spits her disgust: the clams were nothing but breadcrumbs in margarine, the soup flour and water, the veal frozen. Later, my sister will be snapping at her children – why is the house such a mess, why can't they ever pick up their shoes, throw away their soda cans, empty their ashtrays. Glancing at each other, the children will ask how dinner was. 'Great, really terrific!' Later, her husband will tell her she is chewing on the inside of her cheek. 'Your mother upset you,' he will suggest, laying a kind hand on her back. Joy will flare up. 'She didn't! It was a great dinner! If she didn't like it, that's her problem, I could care less! I can't worry about it. I could care less! I could really care less!'

Sometimes my mother whines, sometimes she sulks. She is enraged if my father is not at her side to help her at all times, but often when he puts his hand gently under her elbow to help her over a threshold, she will snatch her arm away and snap at him: 'I'm all right, Ed!' as if he were coercing her into helplessness. She turns her cheek to the kiss he confers upon her before every meal, just after he has helped her into her chair. Often, she sits alone, idle and silent, on the porch of their house, a broad glassed-in room overlooking the lake. But she no longer cries, and she no longer locks herself for days in a darkened room claiming sinus headache, the way she did when I was a teenager.

For many years, she granted me a small power, one that bound me to her irrevocably: when I came to visit her, she would rouse herself, she would talk and laugh and sometimes even forget her sorrow.

This power she granted also to my sister. But for my sister, the business of rousing Mother, entertaining her, trying to make her laugh, was hard work; whereas for me, it was in those days a pleasure. It made me feel strong and full of laughter to laugh with her. She does not laugh any more now though.

She is very lonely but does not try to make friends, and if it is suggested, she snaps 'I don't feel like it!' Other times, when she is feeling better perhaps, she sits in her rocker gazing out at the lake and says, 'There's no lack of drama in my life.' Then she tells me the latest scandal, the latest violence — for among themselves, the cardinals, the big blue jay, the robins, sparrows, ducks, geese, swans, rabbits, chipmunks, possums, squirrels, the neighbour's cat, the tiny red snapper that inhabit the lake, the woods, and the lawn behind my parents' house maintain a steady drama enacted, it seems, for her alone. This drama is full of war and murder and mothering and anxiety. Father ducks — she is sure they are father ducks — squawk angrily at mother ducks anxiously trying to extract their babies from the wire mesh of the neighbour's fence. Male geese — she is sure they are males because they are more aggressive and larger than the others — intimidate the females, and push themselves forward to gobble up all the bread she and my father throw out to them. Her arm is not strong enough to hurl the light crumbs out to where the smaller geese hover hopefully, so she turns on her heel in outrage and refuses to feed them at all. On and on, day after day, contests and resolutions. A family of birds settled in the birdhouse and made a nest, but were so stupid they filled the entire house with twigs, so they could no longer enter it. My mother directed my father as he climbed the ladder and removed some of the stuffing. 'But those birds were really stupid,' my mother announced in contempt. The eggs were all at the bottom of the nest, underneath the stuffing, and they were all cold. She shrugged: 'It was a stupid bird family; it didn't deserve to live.'

She watches the soap opera of nature, over and over again: death and continuation. She finds some rest in this, and occasionally will lift the binoculars to her eyes to observe more closely. But she doesn't hold them long: they are too heavy.

* * *

So when a woman said to me that my mother was strong; when others said 'Your mother is a lovely woman,' I'd simply smile and nod. If you question such statements, people look at you as if they have suddenly discovered you are retarded. Years ago, I would go off by myself and ruminate on such statements: *Is* she strong? What does that mean? How does it show? *Is* she lovely?

I took such judgements as authoritative, and believed they were based on profound perception. I did not then understand that people were in the habit of running around in the world making judgements on all sides without really thinking about what they were saying. I was a very serious child, and believed the state of adulthood was blessed with knowledge and awareness from which I was cut off. I saw adulthood as a special state, people sitting in a brilliantly lit room laughing and talking and nodding their heads, while I stand in the shadows just outside the room unable to understand why they are talking so animatedly about the weather or the traffic, knowing from their vitality and amusement that beneath their ordinary words was a world of hidden meaning, that language was a code known only to the initiated – adults. Oh, in time I learned to read the silences and pauses, learned what the omissions in conversation meant – sex or shame, money or scandal. But I still have trouble with the words. The only word I could place on my mother, surely, without question, is one I have never heard anyone use: in her heart, at her core, my mother is furious.

Still, she was like me too, hanging back in the shadows, timid and alien, knowing herself unwelcome in the adults' room, knowing herself ignorant of it. She wore high shoes too, even higher than mine, but they were in fashion then, and she had the same long spaghetti curls she later visited on me. She would make me sit on the step stool while she heated the curling iron in the gas flame, the same flame she used to singe a chicken, which created a smell similar to that of the singed newspaper she used to twist the iron in before applying it to my limp hair. She would comb off a section of hair, twist it in the evil-smelling iron, then flip it loose and continue around my head until I was judged 'done'. Like the chicken, all its feathers having curled into wisps at the touch of fire, ready to be cooked.

'Did your mommy curl your hair like this?'

'Oh, no, Anastasia.' She said this in what I privately called her 'mad' voice, a tone mingling tiredness and disgust. But then she added mournfully, 'My mother never combed my hair.'

But it was there, in the picture, I insisted: Mommy

at seven, my age exactly, with the same spaghetti curls. And I ran upstairs to get it, to show her. Her shoulders slumped, she grimaced. She was disgusted with me. 'Oh, I don't know, Anastasia, maybe the maid curled it.'

'I don't remember, Anastasia!' She is getting irritated now, as she rolls up the crimped newspaper and stuffs it in the garbage, lays the curling iron on the gas stove to cool, and pours herself another cup of coffee from the dull aluminium drip pot. She sinks into a chair at the kitchen table and lights a cigarette. Clutching the photograph, I leave the room, run to the front room we call the 'porch' and squat on the floor. High black shoes with buttons. They come almost all the way up to her hem. And the shy eyes, the shy smile, the loom of being not-quite-there. This is my mommy. With her is her brother, Eddie, who is nine. He is there, self-possessed, dark, a round mature face. I recognise him, my uncle Eddie whom I love. He is wearing a white suit with knickers and a shirt with a rounded collar. I never saw a white suit like the one in this photograph except when Louis Ferraro died. He had appendicitis, and the teacher made all of us go to his house to pay respects, she said. He was lying in a box in a white suit, with flowers all around him. He was just as fat and tan as ever, but he was dead. His mother and grandmother and all his aunts had black dresses covering their huge bodies, all sitting around the coffin crying. They hardly even looked up, they hardly even answered the teacher. I couldn't understand that: he was only a child, after all. If I had died and was in a box and the teacher came to our house, I knew my mother would be polite and pleasant to the teacher. I thought they were pretending. They couldn't have cared that much about just a child.

When I asked my mother about his white suit, she said it was a Communion suit. Communion suit. That was new. I had heard of union suits, but not *Comm*union suits. I wondered if Eddie's suit was a Communion suit too, and I wanted to ask Mommy, but I knew it would be better if I didn't. I sat on the porch floor, knees together, ankles out, considering. This was a decision I had often to make, but I had no way to predict consequences. I urgently wanted to know if Eddie's suit was a Communion suit too. Finally, I decided to risk it, and jumped up and returned to the kitchen. Mommy was still sitting at the kitchen table, smoking. She was staring at the window, but she didn't seem to be looking at anything. When I entered the room, she didn't move.

'Mommy?' I asked tentatively at the door. 'Is Eddie's suit a Communion suit?'

She looked at me.

I held the photograph out. 'It's white, like Louis Ferraro's.'

She leaned forward and reached out her hand. 'Let me see.' She examined the picture. 'Well, it might have been. But he probably made his First Communion when he was seven – that's what the picture is, it's me in my Communion dress. So his Communion suit was probably too small when he was nine. But maybe Momma made it bigger, Momma was wonderful at that. Or maybe he had a new suit.' The weariness returned to her voice. 'I don't remember.' She returned the picture to me.

I stood transfixed. 'There are Communion dresses too?' My next question would be a big one, and I hesitated. 'What's Communion?' I had been lucky so far, and I knew from experience that I always pushed my luck a little too far. I did this time too.

She burst out tiredly. 'Go and play, Anastasia! Stop bothering me!'

I disappeared.

I went upstairs and lay on my bed. Whenever my mother spoke to me that way, I felt cast into some whirling black place, I felt wrong, I felt all the things she said I was when she was angry with me – selfish, wilful. I felt like a throbbing wart, and I wanted to disappear completely. I wanted to die, and I wondered if she would cry at all, if she would be sorry if I did. Sometimes I thought she would, other times I thought she wouldn't care at all. Yet someplace I knew she did care for me, and that I would understand that if I could only understand her. And so I would think about her, that little girl just my age, and what it was like to be her, and I would remember what she had told me about her life, and the next time I sensed she was in a good mood, I would ask her more about it. I sat up, and leaned back against my pillow. I could feel a certain expression coming on my face. It still does, but now I know what word to label it with: renunciation. I sat there and felt calm, feeling I had a purpose, a cause, an approach – although I did not know those words. I would enter into my mother, and in this way discover the springs of her love.

From Marilyn French's autobiographical novel, *Her Mother's Daughter*, published by William Heinemann.

STEPHANIE DOWRICK
from
RUNNING BACKWARDS
OVER SAND

Zoë Delighty was born on 4 June 1947. She startled
Jane by arriving in a rush and by appearing to lack
the necessary genital confirmation of Jane's belief in
her maleness. It was not that it was difficult for Jane
to adjust to her son being a daughter. Zoë's charms
were immediately clear. She cried a lot, loud lusty
cries, but she responded quickly to Jane's efforts to
soothe her. The rush with which she had been born
made Jane feel, just a little, taken over by Zoë.
Rebecca had taken hours to push steadily down
through the birth canal as Jane breathed and heaved
and held back and pushed, as was appropriate.
Rebecca had behaved as expected, looked as
expected. Jane had been waiting for a Rebecca; a
Rebecca had arrived.

Jane's reaction to the unnamed boy who emerged
a Zoë was initially full of contradictions. This was

the baby who could have been the final straw to send
that camel James out with a broken back. This was
the baby she would have to cope with alone. This
was the baby who was her last chance to have a son.

But Zoë Delighty smiled and dribbled and grew
and held Jane's fingers tightly and nuzzled at Jane's
heavy milky breasts and loved Jane with such passion
that Jane melted, melted into the infant as the infant
melted into her, knowing that she could feel this
tenderness for Zoë with a completeness not possible
when Rebecca was a baby and she had shared her
body and time between shy Rebecca and demanding
James.

She had found it hard, the switch in rhythms from
baby to man, and without being able to acknowledge
it in any conscious way, had simmered with anger
that she was the one who should move, bend to the
demands of one, then back to the demands of
the other. Now, with Zoë, she could sit for hours,
cuddling, feeding, talking, cooing, and when
Rebecca joined them their circle was complete. No
new ball game was asked for.

Twenty-five years later Zoë was to say, for the first
but not the last time, to a group of friends gathered
around a large table, 'My mother breast-fed me for
fifteen months. Life can only go downhill after a start
like that.'

Most people at the table laughed. They thought
she was joking.

Jane stayed in the small wooden house on the bush-
covered hill when James had left for a flat with Caro-
line. She felt safer there, knowing the streets, the

shops, the time the post and milk would be delivered, knowing she could ask neighbours for small favours, to keep an eye on Rebecca, to hold Zoë for a few minutes when Rebecca needed her complete attention. Husbands rarely left their wives in those days, especially when the wife had a small child and another baby on the way. People cast pitying glances at Jane, asked in leaden tones if she was *all right*, and she hated that pity most of all. Hated James for causing her to be the recipient of it. Almost better to be the shamer than the shamed.

But the time passed and Jane obviously coped and the little girls looked lovely in their hand-made clothes: appliquéd dresses with stories on them, knitted cardigans with animals emerging from pockets, brightly coloured shoes, multi-coloured ribbons. Oh yes, Jane could cope.

James sent Jane money. Never enough. How could he, with his new love and first one baby and then quickly another? Plumbing a bottomed pool, scraping, carping, knuckles raw, so many ways to deliver a blow. To bloody.

When Zoë was four and Rebecca almost seven – and able to read as well as any ten-year-old, the teacher told Jane proudly – Jane went back to work. She had worked hard before her marriage to James, and as long as possible before the birth of Rebecca. She had been a teacher, a good one, a woman from the country who understood the ways of city kids, who loved the noise and exhilaration of tiny children beginning to make sense of their world as fuzzy outlines on pages or blackboards became words, magical signposts towards new discoveries.

Now, returning to work, she was exhausted by the

thought of giving herself to any children other than Rebecca and Zoë.

The options to teaching seemed few. She had to be at home for the girls after school, in the shorter holidays at May and August and over the long summer months of Christmas when she would return with them to the farm where she could again be a girl herself. No office working eight to four-thirty would accommodate willingly the reality of her life: total responsibility for two small precious girls.

When she had almost despaired of finding a solution, had tried to animate visions of herself as tea or cleaning lady, as someone who would welcome piles of washing or broken zips to mend, a solution raced to her faster-beating heart, to her working-overtime brain: it had to be right. Without waiting to finish the task at hand, she ran to the local library, poured out her story, her plight, to the woman long familiar in her function as librarian. She would work hard, knew the books, knew the people. Yes, said the librarian. Simply, yes.

The library was almost next door to the school which was prepared to lower its entrance age to absorb bright, loving, thoroughly breast-fed four-year-old Zoë. Zoë, proud of her bigness, eager to be liked, willing to be sat in the front row right under the teacher's eye.

This was the start of an important new period in the lives of Jane and Rebecca and Zoë Delighty. They had a different routine now which began with breakfast together at the big kitchen table, tender with each other at the beginning of a day in which each would be out in her separate world. Occasionally one of them would be cross. Rebecca would often delay Jane and Zoë. Absorbed in a book she would sit, half-dressed, hunched over a page, one shoe on and laced, the other lying beside her, and would grump and grumble when Zoë or Jane would screech that it was time to go, time to walk down the two long rows of houses, past a short burst of shops, each with its wooden awning, protection against inflated drops of tropical rain, to school and library.

In the evenings, just sometimes, Jane went out and the big girl from next door came in to sit with Zoë and Rebecca. Jane went to pottery classes, to films, to occasional parties when she would look and smell especially delicious. More often friends came to her, especially her dearest friend, Maria. She came more than once a week, glowing with pleasure at being with Jane, apparently even with pleasure at being with Jane's daughters. Their conversation was seamless, a flow of gossip, politics, jokes, reassurance. Words begun by one then picked up by the other then returned, deepened in meaning, or lightened and bounced: women's talk.

The sound of the women's voices was good for the little girls to hear. They could have stayed to listen in the kitchen, or out on the back porch, wherever the women were, but didn't need to. They felt very little curiosity about most of what was discussed, and no anxiety. Maria came, kissed them all with loud smacking kisses, distributed chocolate-covered buzz bars or sticky yellow lumps of hokey-pokey, talked, laughed, kissed again and left.

James also came. Every other Saturday his old Austin would pull up outside. Jane would go out to stand on the edge of the footpath as he emerged, tall and awkward, from the car. On fine days she would stand there with him, chatting before he came in. On wet days the two adults would talk in the kitchen while Rebecca and Zoë played, tried to play or to sink more deeply into a book, in their shared bedroom. James and Jane rarely laughed and their talk had a scratchy quality to it which reminded Zoë of fingernails on a blackboard.

Jane wanted to make James' visits pleasant for the children, perhaps pleasant for James too so he wouldn't give up coming. And she continued to care that he came.

She would cook special meals for when he returned with the girls from their outings. Zoë, who noticed such things, knew that her mother made certain dishes only when her father, or another male guest, was to be present. Her friends' mothers did that too. A kitchen peopled by a woman and assorted kids had an atmosphere very different from that where a woman, a man and assorted kids sat together. Table manners, table settings, especially table conversation and atmosphere changed when there was a Dad around. The atmosphere grew more charged, energy flowing in lines rather than in circles; rights and wrongs fought it out, rather than collapsing in a muddle in the middle.

Zoë liked it that their Dad came only every other Saturday. She quite enjoyed the outings he took them on. There was nothing to object to unless you count a certain boredom, sensed but not fully understood by Zoë and Rebecca, provoked by his inability to get the point of their true-life accounts, by his failure to respond to the games of fantasy at which they and Jane effortlessly excelled.

Between those Father-Days, Rebecca and Zoë almost always had Jane to themselves. Maria didn't count. She added to the atmosphere they enjoyed. She was so like Jane: warm, soft, funny, caressing easily, listening with real interest.

Friday nights before James' visits took on a special quality. The small town close to the large city where they lived itself seemed large and impressive to Zoë and Rebecca. It had one main street where the 'big' shops were. None of these shops had more than two storeys, most had only one, but their floor space appeared vast. The girls and Jane had a routine that allowed for only slight variations. After school and library and home-for-tea they set out, not in their usual direction, but cutting through the churchyard. Each girl held one of Jane's hands, and her head would turn first one way and then the other, and sometimes straight down as the girls leant across her to talk and to giggle at each other. They looked remarkably alike, this woman and her daughters: firm bodies, dark hair bouncing in short unruly curls, light eyes – blue behind glasses for Jane and Rebecca, green for Zoë – bright faces, not pretty but mobile, curious and open. All three talked a lot, excited by the outing, familiar though it would be.

The churchyard contained a number of graves, mostly very old from the beginning of the settlement of the town in the later years of the nineteenth century. Brave English people buried in the new land they had come to with such high hopes for better lives. Dead now, anyway. A new cemetery lay just outside the town, a mat of tended green broken by shiny, ugly slabs with an occasional concrete erection tor-

tured into angel shape. Most people preferred that
distance, preferred not to be reminded of cold grey
marble over deep dark dirt hugging pale, unlit bones.

On how much better ashes. Light blowy ashes.
Translucent, soft, disappearing from the ends of fingers. Now you see them, now you dont. Gone for
ever. High, high. Sky high.

Jane's warm live fingers are caught on either side by
Rebecca and Zoë as they make the first of their ritual
stops. Yvonne Lee is in Zoë's class. She speaks English
for her mother who presides over their shop, nodding, smiling encouragement at the customers but
totally reliant during her husband's frequent absences
on this sombre girl, her daughter, who has managed
to learn what is for Mrs Lee the eternally unlearnable
English. The regular customers point, pick things up,
or wait for Yvonne's help, tiny Yvonne, tinier than
Zoë despite two extra years, confident of her place
at her mother's side in the life of the shop. Poor Mrs
Lee. It is her clever stock-filling which makes of this
small place a magic cavern: birds on sticks, paper
lanterns, kites, exquisitely embroidered towels and
clothes, boxes smelling of camphor. Most thrilling of
all are the objects which can be wound into life, to
whirl, to walk, to cluck, to coo. Mrs Lee's smiles are
lively too, but what does she feel with no adult chat
to break up yawning days?

From the long racks under the high ceiling hang
the most dazzling of the whirling, whizzing, cooing
objects. Sometimes, when she sees favourite customers arriving, Mrs Lee will drag a small step ladder
to the centre of the shop floor, will climb on to it
and wind up the objects, making a wild cacophonous

display which enchants the onlookers and perhaps Mrs Lee herself who laughs and bobs on the steps of the ladder.

On the tables beneath are the more practical items to be bought on everyday occasions after your eyes have soaked in the glories above. Here are the rubbers, pencil-sharpeners in all kinds of disguise, pencils and pens and small and large notepads. There is always some item that Jane or one of the girls needs.

Zoë is respectful as Yvonne takes the money. The Chinese girl barely reaches the till but delivers back perfect change with a seriousness that separates her totally from the classmate who's only too pleased if Zoë nudges her through the hard words at reading time.

There are other Chinese store-owners in the small town. Mrs Lee's own sister is married to the town's greengrocer. She'll be dragging and heaving sacks of onions, of potatoes, of sweet purplish lumps of kumara, lifting boxes of watermelon, of peaches, grapes and apples throughout the nine months of repeated pregnancies. Her husband's brother sells fish and chips, fish freshly dipped in batter then fried in huge vats of boiling oil while customers wait, wet-mouthed in the narrow, hot shop, for their precious parcel wrapped in newspaper which can be torn across the top to dive into the goodies beneath. But even the most delicious fruit and vegetables, or fish and chips, can't match the magic of Mrs Lee's cavern.

Zoë loves Mrs Lee, and though she is made shy by her limited comprehension that Mrs Lee cannot think or speak in English, she makes a special point, each visit, of smiling hesitantly but firmly at the woman, occasionally telling her things, noting Mrs

Lee's careful attention and sure that some of what she's saying is reaching her. She is rewarded, always, with a returned smile and a nodding bow.

Sometimes Mrs Lee will rustle behind the counter, producing, always scrupulously fair, two tiny goodies; strange sweets which taste as odd as their smell; brilliantly coloured fluffy birds, wonderful to stroke; sticks of incense which Jane will light when they get home and which will allow Zoë, eyes pressed tightly shut, to imagine herself all the way to Hong Kong where Yvonne was born.

Whatever the outcome of the visit to Mrs Lee's 'Hong Kong Paradise', Zoë is always surprised, always enchanted. They all say thank you, thank you and goodbye and see you soon. They bow and smile just as Mrs Lee does. They want her to feel at home.

Spirits lifting, spirits soaring. Zoë remembers: the smell of Jane, the touch of Jane. Safe at her side, my face rubs against the pocket of her grey flannel coat and when she bends down over me her scratchy scarf tickles and I push it away and she rubs me on the top of my head and I look up into her face and I see her wide mouth move and I see her eyes behind her glasses do a little jiggle as they look at me and I am safe safe safe in my world and I swing back on my arm, swing back behind her, make my arm long to hide these giant's feelings I have inside me that I don't have names for but they make me giggle and now I press my giggle into her back, my face against her soft bum and she can feel my hot dragon breath sieved through her clothes and she turns around and kneels down so that our faces are at equal height and she looks at me and she has those giant's feelings too, I can tell I can see them and she doesn't know what they are either and she laughs her lovely laugh and calls my Zoë name, Zoë my zoo creature she says, and she puts her face in my neck and snuggles beneath my ear until I shriek and laugh and then she stands up and we all walk on. My mother, my sister, and I.

From Stephanie Dowrick's autobiographical novel, *Running Backwards Over Sand*, published by Penguin Books.

MARY DALY
from
OUTERCOURSE

My parents had always given me many beautiful books as presents, especially on holidays. So the World of Glowing Books somehow entered the realm of my imagination very early and became a central focus of the Quest to be a philosopher. More than once in high school I had dreams of wondrous worlds – of being in rooms filled with colourful glowing books. I would wake up in a state of great ecstasy and knowing that this was *my* World, where I belonged.

During that early adolescent time I also Discovered the 'celestial gleam' of nature. Since my father was a travelling salesman who sold icecream freezers, I sometimes went with him on drives into the country when he visited his customers' icecream stands. My awakening to the transcendental glowing light over meadows and trees happened on some of these trips. Other Moments of contact with Nature involved knowing the Call of the Wild from the mountains and purple skies and the sweet fresh smell of snow.

These invitations from Nature to my adolescent spirit were somehow intimately connected with the Call of the World Glowing Books. My life was suffused with the desire for a kind of Great Adventure that would involve touching and exploring these strange worlds that had allowed me to glimpse their wonders and Lust for more.

I was reasonably well equipped to follow this seemingly improbably, not fully articulated, yet crystal clear Call. For one thing I was endowed with insufferable stubbornness – a quality which never failed me. I also had the gift of being at least fifty per cent oblivious of society's expectations of me as a 'normal' young woman and one hundred per cent resistant to whatever expectations I did not manage to avoid noticing. For example, I never had the slightest desire to get married and have children. Even in elementary school and in the absence of any Feminist movement I had felt that it would be intolerable to give up my own name and become 'Mrs' something or other. It would obviously be a violation of mySelf. Besides, I have always really *liked* my name. I wouldn't sell it for anything. A third asset was a rock bottom self-confidence and Sense of Direction which, even in the bleakest periods, have never entirely deserted me.

Looking back, I recognise that all of these assets were gifts from my extraordinary mother. For one thing, she had always made it clear to me that she had desired only one child, and that one a daughter. I was exactly what she wanted, and all she wanted.

How she managed to arrange this I was never told. At any rate my father seemed to have no serious objection. For another thing, I cannot recall that she ever once – even once – tried to promote the idea that I should marry and have a family, although she often said that she was very happily married, and indeed this seemed to be the case.

* * *

Perhaps the most remarkable inheritance bestowed on me by my mother was the flood of encouraging messages about *my work*. She was a meticulous house-keeper, but she thoroughly discouraged me from helping with any of the housework. Whenever I made one of my half-hearted offers to do the dishes she would invariably say: 'No, you go and do your own work, dear.' What that meant to me when I was eight, nine and fifteen was, essentially, that I had to find out what my work was, and go do it.

* * *

Because my mother said 'Go do your own work, dear.' Oh, that woman! Because she chose me and because she said that: 'Go, do your own work,' she sent off a Time bomb, that woman. Because she gave me the taste for Ecstasy, the Lust for It. Because I have It still, and more, and more.

. . . Open the door. And run out, Mary, run. Hug the Green, the Green Grass. Fly with the winds, rush with the waters. Light Her Fire.

And Oh, the desire, the desire for all of It. For the Moment that is Now, Expanding Now. The Now that holds and releases the past, that touches the future. The Now that they can't know about – the undead vampire men, the bio-robots gone berserk, the leaders.

Run right into the Now. There is so much room (no room for gloom). It is so open here, there, everywhere. So full of the sweet, fresh smells of earth and air. Just dare!

From *Outercourse/The Be-Dazzling Voyage/Containing Recollections From M₁ Logbook of a Radical Feminist Philosopher/(Be-ing an Account of my Time/Space Travels and Ideas/Then, Again, Now and How)*, published by The Women's Press.

CATHERINE COOKSON
from
OUR KATE

My aunt Sarah and my mother went into 'place' when they were twelve years old. Of course they had done work long before this, but it was mixed up with school – that is when they attended, for sending three children to school meant threepence a week and you could make a dinner for that with a penn'orth of pot stuff (vegetables), a penn'orth of peas, beans and barley, and a penn'orth of pieces. What did it matter if there was sawdust sticking to the black congealed blood on the meat or that it was just a piece of the beast's lungs – it made a dinner.

They had also begged bread from door to door. I used to envy my mother having experienced these things because I longed for such poverty that there would be no money left for drink. My mother used to tell me of being sent out to beg for bread one day – she was not the only one begging at that time in Jarrow. Her feet were bare and bleeding, the calves of her legs split with keens. At one house a compassionate woman took her in and gave her a pair of boots and stockings, and she went home, forgetting about the bread. Her delight in the boots, although her feet were paining even worse from their pressure on the keens, was short lived, for her mother took them immediately to the 'In and Out'. It was an appropriate name, for you would pawn, say, your man's suit on a Monday to meet the rent and if you hadn't the money to get it out on the Friday you would take in something else to help retrieve it. Brass candlesticks, mats, fire irons, even the stone dish you baked the bread in. One thing was always going in to get the other out.

My mother's first spell of actual service was in a house in Stanhope Road, Tyne Dock. I think they were butchers. There were four sons, and the washing was colossal. She couldn't reach the top of the poss-tub to wield the poss-stick, a great wooden beater on four legs, three to four foot high, so the woman had a stool made for her. She did all the housework, all the washing and all the ironing. She worked from half-past six in the morning until late at night, with half a day off a fortnight, and all for half-a-crown a week, usually subbed a month or two ahead. She stayed there a year. The tale of my mother's first place stayed in the front of my mind even as a child, and when I went into service I thought how lucky I was to be treated so differently. But only for a very short time.

I was born when Kate was twenty-four and the life she was made to endure because of me would have driven anyone less strong not only to drink but

into the madhouse. The cruelty of the bigoted poor
has to be witnessed to be believed. It has to be lived
with to be understood.

When my mother, sick to depths of her soul, as I
know now she was, had to come home from 'her
place' and say she was going to have a baby, the
fathar, as he was always called, was for killing her –
she had committed the unforgivable sin. Yet when I
was born and she had milk fever and her breasts
swelled to bursting, the fathar was supposed to have
saved her life by sucking the milk from them. It
seems incredible to me that she should have looked
upon this act as something almost heroic for, remembering him as I do, I can see that he would have
enjoyed this operation – he was a frustrated, licentious
man. His antidote against this, which the ailing health
of me grandma could not alleviate, was drink and a
dirty tongue, which he used against all women. Yet
I must say that only on rare occasions did he let
himself go in my presence, at least when he was
sober. I feel grateful to him for this, for he had been
known to make even the toughest women in the
New Buildings blush.

As the years went on I think that of the two, me
grandma was harder on Kate than the fathar, because,
when coming home from place on her rare days off,
if she'd attempt to take me in her arms me grandma
would grab me from her, re-arrange my clothes and
almost dust me down, as if Kate's hands had contami-
nated me in some way.

At the time she met my father she was working in
an inn in Lamesley. She was working in the bar, and
had been for two or three years. Her sister, Mary,
who was three years younger, was a housemaid, and

a very haughty, hot-tempered housemaid at that. I am not quite sure of the name of the owners of the inn at that time but I do know that the daughter was Miss Jenny. Kate often spoke of her. Also of the pitmen who used to take the long trek past the inn to the mine, and on pay day, which was once a fortnight, have a blow up in the bar and a pay up for the odd pints that had gone on the slate. She must have been a favourite with them, for she was an attractive woman in those days, gay, warm, large-hearted.

My father, I understand, first set eyes on her when she served him in the saloon.

Kate never told my anything about him until six years before she died. It was my Aunt Mary who, when I was sixteen, gave me the sketchy outline of my beginnings and set up in my mind an inordinate pride, a sense of false superiority and a burning desire to meet this wonderful creature who had shocked me into being. This man. This gentleman. Oh, yes, he was a gentleman. My Aunt Mary stated this with emphasis. She had no love for her sister, Kate. Later in life when Kate became the object of her scorn, she still remained jealous of her, for people liked Kate, loved her in spite of everything. Mary did not have a nature that one could love, and when she imparted this news to me it was to hurt Kate, make me more ashamed of her. Yet deep in me I knew that my Aunt Mary wasn't a patch on 'Our Kate'. But Mary was often kind to me, it was only her scorn of Kate that made me dislike her. Anyway, Mary said this gentleman went head over heels as soon as he saw Kate.

What did this gentleman do for a living?

Nobody has ever been able to tell me.

How did Mary know he was a gentleman?

Well, he wore a black coat with an astrakhan collar. He had a high hat and carried a silver mounted walking stick and black kid gloves, like 'The Silver King', she said. 'And he spoke different . . . lovely.'

For two years the gentleman courted Kate. He did not come regularly but when he did he took her out, arranging his visits to her day off. She looked at no one else in the way she did at him. She was deeply in love. What did she expect from this association? She never said. But, knowing her level-headedness, I feel that she knew from the beginning that it was hopeless and therefore she kept him in his place, except for once; and once was enough. It seems pitiable to me at this distance that it wasn't until she was twenty-three that she first went with a man. I say first; it was the one and only time she had this kind of association with my father, and it's more pitiable still that she never had this association with anyone else until over sixteen years later when she married David McDermott, because she was of a loving nature. I can feel myself getting angry when I think that she was branded as a fallen woman – and you needed to make a mistake only once and give evidence of it in order to acquire this prefix in those days – whilst today girls still at school indulge in intimacy for kicks. If I hadn't stopped believing in God this injustice would surely have acted as a springboard against believing in a benevolent father, a controller of destinies, someone who has our welfare at heart, for such a deity must surely have had his favourites, and Kate wasn't one of them. Her taking to drink, her servitude to her mother and stepfather in a house hardly ever without lodgers, the persecution, through love, or lust, of her half-brother, the indignities and slights she had to put up with, the undermining and ruining of her moral fibre, can all be laid at the door of one ecstatic moment.

My bitterness on this point is not for myself because I realise now that in being part of 'the gentleman' — and I have my tongue in my cheek even as I write the word — I have a great deal to be thankful for, for he provided the norm at which I aimed. It was him in me that pushed and pulled me out of the drabness of my early existence. It was from him that I got the power to convey awareness, this painful sensitivity, without which what I sensed in others would have remained an untranscribable mass of feelings. Yet should I be thankful? Wouldn't it have been much easier for me if, having been born sixteen years later, I had inherited David McDermott's utter placidity? With this trait, and a touch of my mother's sense of humour, life would have been a straight line track, no sharp bends, no uphill pulls and . . . no summit.

* * *

At the time we moved to the New Buildings our Kate and my Aunt Sarah and Aunt Mary were in place, and strangely enough they had not been informed of the move. I first became aware of our Kate one night as I played under the lamp near the top end of the street. I had a rope tied to the lamp post and was dizzying round on the end of it singing 'When I was going to Strawberry Fair, singing, singing buttercups and daisies, I met a lady taking the air for a day. Her eyes were blue, she had gold in her hair and she was going to Strawberry Fair, singing, singing buttercups and daisies, singing, singing tral-la-la-la-la' when out of the shadow beyond the rim of light emerged our Kate. I stopped my dizzying and stared at her, while the rope went limp in my hand. To me she looked beautiful – tall, dressed in a grey costume, with beautiful hair on which was perched a big hat. She took hold of my arm and shook me from my daze, saying, 'Where are they?' She had arrived at the old house in Leam Lane to find it empty and had become very distressed, for, poor as the house was, it was a focal point. She feared the disintegration of the home then as she was to fear it until the fathar died. I think she feared it for him more than for herself, for John McMullen had a deep secret terror, he was afraid of ever being homeless and having to end his days in the work-house. Vaguely I remember her going upstairs into the new house, and there going for me grandma while the tears ran down her face. Me grandma said, 'Well, I just couldn't get down to writing. And besides, there was the writing paper and envelope to buy and the stamp, and I hadn't got it.'

I remember liking our Kate to come home, for she always brought parcels of food with her. At this time she was working in a baker's shop in Chester-le-Street, baking the bread and cakes, and her money, as ever, was booked weeks ahead. She took most of it in the form of groceries and what was over she tipped up on her visits home. Mary and Sarah were not called upon to do this, but then they had not committed a sin, a sin which had to be fed and clothed. When they were young girls they had had to 'stump up' their money, but as the years went on they did this less and less. Me grandma was a foolishly generous woman and a bad housekeeper and Kate used to be infuriated, she told me, when they lived in Tyne Dock – not in Leam Lane but in Nelson Street I think it was – and she would come home from her half-a-crown or three shillings a week place to find sponging neighbours being feasted with broth, and brisket, and beer, when perhaps only two days before, following a distracted appeal, she had sent home another subbed-week's wages. This never happened at the New Buildings, but there were a thousand and one other ways me grandma could squander senselessly the little money that came into the house. Yet she herself didn't drink much.

From this particular night when Kate came consciously on to my horizon she was never to leave it.

It is true to say that Kate never left the house to return to her place with anything except a return ticket in her purse. Should the fathar or Jack be in the house, which inevitably they would be when there wasn't any money floating around, she couldn't see them doing without a drink. She was a big soft-hearted goof. It was strange, too, but she rarely touched drink then.

In these days working men, should their wives be ill, will set to and see to the house, but in those days a man went out to work and that, to his mind, was enough; the house and all in it was the woman's task, and it lowered a man's prestige if he as much as lifted a cup. The lower down the working class scale you were, the more this rule applied. Even many years later I heard me granda describe a man as the nappy washer because he had seen to the house when his

wife was confined to bed with her first baby. The
neighbours usually did this chore with or without
pay, more often without, because in those days neighbours did not expect to be paid. Both me granda
and me uncle Jack would have let their clothes go
rotten on their backs before they would have washed
them; as for cooking a meal, even if hey had known
how to, they wouldn't have lowered themselves to
the level of the fire, or the gas stove. Man's rightful
standing in his house was a thing to be guarded, to
be fought for; no weakness or emotions or kindly
instincts must touch it. Our men didn't even mend
the boots, Kate had to do that. With the last on her
knees and a mouthful of tacks she would hammer
away, soling and heeling the big ugly working boots,
and after a day that would have worn out two
women.

So there came a time, because me grandma became
ill – this was shortly following the night Kate pulled
me from the lamp post – that she had to give up her
limited liberty and come home to be Jack-of-all-
trades. Had there not been myself to use as a hold
over her she might have refused, yet I doubt it,
knowing Kate.

She worked for everybody, and anybody. Besides
nursing me grandma and attending to fleeting lodgers, she went out and did days washing or cleaning,
paper-hanging and painting, ceilings and staircases,
she even replaced window sashes and whole window
frames and for never more than three shillings a day.
So it is little wonder that the hopelessness of her life,
looming so large before her, drove her to an antidote
to enable her to go through with it. Yet her ready
smile, her joking and pleasant disposition, never gave

away what she felt about some of her employers. It was only years later that I knew how she had hated doing for 'those worse than yourself'.

Besides having a lovely face she was beautifully built, with a skin the equal of which I have never seen, pure milk and roses. She had two great azure blue eyes, with dark curving brows. Her hair was brown and abundant and she had a wide generous mouth full of strong teeth with which she cracked brazil nuts until she was seventy. But it was the mouth that showed her weakness, with a top lip full to slackness. She was of a dominant nature, yet this was balanced by an innate softness; she was very forgiving, was Kate. She had in her a sense of humour to which she gave rein on every occasion. She was more beautiful when she was serious; there was a depth to her when she was serious, and it was the depth in her that attracted me.

I never knew her to be without swollen ankles, but this did not mar a woman in those days for the skirts came down to the top of the shoes. Her left ankle had been swollen, she told me, since she was a small child and it caused her left foot to flap slightly inwards as she walked, but her walk was stately, yet tripping – she always seemed to be on the point of a run. Constitutionally she was as strong as a horse, yet in some strange way this constitution refused to carry drink, for, from the first glass of spirit she drank, her personality changed for the worse. After three glasses she became, not our Kate, but someone of whom I was deeply ashamed, whom in my early years I came to fear, then hate; then wish dead, yet all the time loved, loved because she was the only thing that was mine; even while I disowned her in my mind I loved her. This clash of emotions presented itself to me for the first time one Saturday afternoon.

I had been to the penny matinee at the Crown in Hudson Street, Tyne Dock. I loved the pictures because at the pictures not only did I see, through my half-covered eyes, beautiful ladies being tied on to railway lines, where they lay in agony from one Saturday afternoon until the next waiting for the trains to come crashing over them, or the hero, who had already escaped death countless times, at last caught and tied to within an inch of a madly spinning saw, but I also saw gracious ladies and gentlemen in big houses, surrounded by cars, horses and servants, exactly like the pictures I conjured up on the wall when I turned my face away from life, away from all the nasty things. I never covered my eyes with my fingers and peered through the penumbra of fleshy light when I looked at pictures like this at the Crown but I would stare wide-eyed and open-mouthed into the wonder of another world, and because of this other world I didn't like Ben Turpin, or Keystone Cops or, later still, daft people like Charlie Chaplin. Charlie Chaplin always filled me with embarrassment. The poor desolate creatures he portrayed were too near to something inside myself. No, I never, even when I grew up, liked Charlie Chaplin. I just liked pictures of . . . ladies and gentlemen.

At four o'clock on this particular Saturday I came out of the Crown and was walking in a happy daze down the Dock Bank. I was walking backwards, which I often did when I was happy, and I turned swiftly on hearing my name called and bumped my nose right into a tram standard, to the great amusement of some of the onlookers. Then through my dazed vision I saw, coming across the road from the direction of Bede Street, our Kate, and there was something about her that startled me. Something in her walk. I thought I was seeing things funny because I had bumped my nose. She looked down at me, smiling widely, and her eyes looked smoky and she clutched my hand as we went down the Bank towards the tram terminus. When there, she began to talk and laugh. Her talk was thick and her words fuddled, and her laugh made me lower my lids. And it came to me, in a sickening revelation, that our Kate was drunk. She walked up and down as we waited for the tram, and as I looked downwards I saw her left foot give a more abandoned fling to itself when it left the ground. This action of her left foot was scarcely noticeable when she hadn't taken anything, but once she touched spirit it went not only to her head but to her left foot. This was the first time I became aware that there isn't a part of body or mind that remains unaffected by spirits.

* * *

[Throughout her life, Catherine Cookson's relationship with 'Our Kate' was stormy. After David McDermott died, Our Kate's drinking got worse. Her visits to Catherine in the later part of her life were a pleasure, but also a strain].

For six years Kate had been visiting me, and each year her visits grew longer, until they lasted for three months. Always during her stay I got her her daily beer, and never once did she ask for, or mention, whisky. This spoke plainly of her power of control,

which she could use if she liked. I know now that
there were times when she was staying with me when
she must have gone through hell, so great was her
craving.

Following each visit, I always got a letter saying,
'Oh, lass, only four walls to look at and no garden;
and no you, or Tom.' She had by this time become
very attached to Tom.

Twice during her long stays she was ill and in bed
for six weeks at a time, and strangely I enjoyed nursing her. When her dominant character was low and
I knew there was no possibility of her slipping out,
she became Our Kate to me, the nice Our Kate.

But as the years went on, and although there were
three hundred miles between us now, the burden of
her still weighed on me, for I was living in dread
of the day when, not being able to look after herself,
I would, to use her own phraseology, be saddled with
her.

When the final day of testing came in 1953 and I
went North, I found her in a deplorable state. She
had swelled to enormous proportions. She had heart
trouble, dropsy, and cancer of the stomach, the last
she was unaware of, and she had been drinking heavily, paying someone to bring it in for her. Dr Carstairs
gave her a short time to live. Like me granda, she
had a fear of hospital, so there was nothing for it but
to bring her back with me.

What strengthened and helped me during this time
was Tom's moral support. Although he knew to what
depths of mental distress she had brought me, and
the daily irritations in store for himself – one of
which was her cooking, for she took it as an insult
if her great stacked plates of gravy covered food

weren't eaten – he said, 'You must bring her home.'
And I knew I must, and for good, for my conscience
was loud in me, telling me that whatever I went
through with her now would be nothing to what I
would suffer if I didn't make this final effort.

After a journey by train sleeper, and ambulance, I
brought her home for the last time. She was ill, very
ill, and when at last I had her in bed in her old room
and I looked at her, I thought, thank God it won't
be for long, then was immediately horrified that I
could think this way. I stared pityingly down at the
great balloon of water that her body had become, at
the faded blue of her eyes, and the colour of her
nose, bulbous now. There was no beauty left, not
even the beauty of age. And then she took my hand.
With the tears running down her face she held it to
her cheek as she said, 'Aw, lass, thank God I'm home.
I'm home, I'm home. Aw, me lass. Aw, me lass, God's
good. He's brought me home to die. Every night
when I've said me prayers I've asked him to bring
me home.' Strange, but she did say her prayers every
night, and stranger still that she should consider her
home was wherever I was.

I said to her, 'You are not going to die . . . Mam,
you are going to live to be happy.' I had called her
mam for the first time.

And she did live, and she was happy. For three
years we lived together, and for most of the time there
was happiness. There were the ordinary irritations of
life, more so when she was getting about as she did
sometimes in the morning – she had to be in bed
most days by two o'clock – because she always wanted
to do the cooking, and the name of Gayelord Hauser

affected her like a red rag to a bull, for our eating habits for some years had been guided by his cookery books.

Only twice did she express any desire to go out, and on the first occasion she stopped abruptly outside a bar door and said as abruptly, 'I won't be a few minutes, I just want a half, just a half.' Sickness overwhelmed me again, and bitterness. I knew she would down a couple of doubles and have a flat flask in her bag and all within a few minutes. But following this I realised the agony the craving caused her, and decided that I must get her some spirits, at least once or twice a month. And so, on the quiet, I would bring her in a quarter bottle of whisky, saying, 'Hide that,' for Tom wasn't supposed to know anything about it. And very often he didn't for he was strongly against her having it; beer yes, and brandy, which the doctor had ordered, but not whisky. She hated brandy. Oh, the look on her face when I would give her the bottle. 'Aw, thanks lass, thanks lass.' She would be happy, and laughing, and gay for days.

But the most important thing during this period was that we came to know one another. We talked openly about the past for the first time in our lives. And once she said to me, 'I've never understood you, lass. It's come to me that I've never understood you. Years ago I used to think you had the making of an upstart, and funny, I wanted you to be an upstart, because it proved to me you were different. But you were different from the day you were born. You were like him, you didn't belong to the North or anything in it.' Here she was wrong. 'But you were no upstart, you were too straight and honest for that, and you never rejected me.' (If she could only have seen into my mind and heart.) 'I once heard tell that Taggart Smith said to you in the New Buildings when you were leaving home to go into place that time, that you should make a clean break from us an' that you would never make anything of yourself if you kept in with us. It was me she meant. I've never born malice to anybody in me life but I found it hard to forgive her for that. But you did make something of yourself. There's nobody in the place risen like you have, an' you didn't disown us to do it.'

* * *

I have written my tale in the room where Kate died. The roses are tapping on the window again and her presence is strong about me. I look towards the corner where her bed stood and she is smiling at me.

'You'll feel better now lass.'

'You think so?'

'Sure of it.'

'I've tried to be fair.'

'You were always fair, lass, always. And you haven't put down half that happened, you never need worry about not being fair. But because you've learned to forgive, things will settle in you now.'

'I don't know. I've still a long way to go . . . and, well there's my religion. I want a religion, something that I can believe in, not a denomination, a religion.'

'It'll come, lass, never doubt. Remember that piece of poetry you read to me once by somebody with a name like, like ammonia.'

'You mean Aumonier.'

'Yes, that's him. Well, say it now, and say it every

day and it'll come true. Believe me lass, it'll come true.'

I will seek Beauty all my days

Within the dark chaos of a troubled world I will
   seek and find some Beauteous Thing.

From eyes grown dim with weeping will shine a
   Light
   to guide me, and in Sorrow's Hour
   I shall behold a great High Courage.

I shall find the wonder of an infinite Patience,
   and a quiet Faith in coming Joy and Peace.

And Love will I seek in the midst of Discord, and
   find swift eager hands out-stretched in
   welcome.

I will seek Beauty all my days, and in my quest
   I shall not be dismayed.

I   SHALL   FIND   GOD

Goodbye, Kate, and thank you for giving me life.

From *Our Kate*, published by Little, Brown.

MAY SARTON,
'A WILD GREEN PLACE'

'Tell me about Wales. Tell me what it was like,' I used to beg my mother when I was a child. I never tired of hearing her descriptions of the wild green place, hearing those bits and pieces of a story that I did not come to know in its entirety until several years after her death. Then I found out what 'it was like' – what it was really like, the whole story written down in her own hand and left among her papers for someone (or no one) to find, not a tale told to a little daughter but the pinning down once and for all of a complex experience that had haunted her. It has been like putting one of those tightly curled Japanese flowers into a glass of water and watching it open, for this early memory of my mother's seems to reveal in essence the flowering of a lifetime.

My mother belonged to the Elwes family, of Suffolk, England. Gervase Elwes, her father, was a civil engineer and responsible for laying out railways, roads and bridges in India, Spain and Canada, and therefore he was often away from home for long periods of time. I have gathered that my grandmother loved him almost to the exclusion of her two children, Hugh and Mabel. It apparently never occurred to her, when she and her husband set out for Canada (where Gervase Elwes had a job working on the extension of the Winnipeg waterworks), that it might seem strange to abandon these two – nine and seven, respectively – for two long years. Hugh was sent to boarding school, of course, and Mabel was shipped off to a small farm in Wales. No doubt the idea of the farm came from her father, a sensitive and understanding man, who had been troubled by his little girl's constant painful war with society as represented by a nanny, by any rule or regulation, by any 'planned activity'. Perhaps wild Wales may have seemed to this imaginative creature an entirely suitable landscape for his wild little daughter to roam in, happily set free from all that had bruised and harassed her in the genteel atmosphere of home. She was to be given the gift of solitude at this very early age, and though it would seem to us now a rather daring gift, how right he was! I know what a radiance of remembered happiness crossed my mother's face when she spoke of Wales, as of some lost Paradise, and what this long period of solitary communion with nature did for one who was always a discerning and passionate observer of flowers, trees and animals – one who would later have to remake her home many times among strangers, and twice even change her nationality. But the English woman in her accompanied every change, translating itself into gardens wherever she went, into the creation of beautiful surroundings, and, too, into a kind of impassioned solitariness. So what happened to her at seven in Wales was a preparation for much that was to happen later on.

Gervase Elwes and his wife were not wholly aware of the particular environment into which they put their daughter so casually when they went off to Canada. What happened was that at the last minute the family with whom all arrangements had been made for Mabel, was unable to take the child; the Elweses, on the brink of departure, had to accept the word of these comparative strangers that they had found ideal substitutes. But the original family, as it turned out, was simply doing some poor relatives a good turn by providing them with a little extra income. Mabel's foster parents turned out to be two women − 'Grannie' of the kind wrinkled face and kind hands, and 'Aunt Mollie', her daughter, a tall, high-strung woman with eyes as blue as a jay's feathers, who it appears, took an instant dislike to 'the rich little girl'. Even Grannie, of whom Mabel grew so fond, showed her no real affection until later. They were hard, primitive people, who perhaps regarded the child as primitive peoples regard 'the foreigner' (she was English, they were Welsh) − as someone primarily to be exploited. Even so, it is hard to comprehend why one of the first things the two women did was to take away all Mabel's best clothes and give them to a nearby relative. There is, curiously enough, no reference to this astonishing cruel behaviour in my mother's written document. But though my mother did not choose to remember it when she came to write the story, it made an indelible impression on me as a child − so much so that I feel forced to place it in the record here. I remember very well my impotent rage at not being able to go back in time and tell those two women what I thought of them. I remember begging my mother to assure me that when her parents finally came back and rescued her, they did something violent and drastic, but she could not recollect that they did. Perhaps Eleanor and Gervase Elwes ended by feeling pity rather than anger, though my grandmother's irascibility was well known, and my memories of her include her shaking a fierce umbrella at a carter whose horse looked underfed, and threatening him in no uncertain terms with the law. At any rate, the whole story left in my mind a sense of incompleteness, of justice not done, until I read my mother's mature judgement of it and began to understand that, in comparison with all that followed of so much deeper human significance, this initial harshness may have seemed irrelevant.

Besides, memory distils the essence, and the essence of this whole experience for my mother was being alone in the country and all that that meant to the person she was.

Photographs of Mabel Elwes at this time show a pretty child with large, wide apart grey eyes, at the same time mischievous and dreamy, and light chestnut curls piled up on her head. There is plenty of stubborn will in the mouth and chin. For her, Wales meant first and always escape – escape into lush meadows and an orchard in deep grass, and, above all, escape to the lovely shallow river, which ran bronzing over flat stones. At one place, she found a grassy bank quite close to the water, where she could lie for hours on her stomach and let the current flow through her hands like a constantly renewed spell; it was a forbidden game, and all the more delightful for that reason. In the orchard, a step up the hillside from the vegetable garden just back of the farm, lived Daisy, a greige-coloured Jersey cow. Daisy allowed the little girl certain privileges; for instance, she could lie against the cow's warm flank when she rested in the shade at noon, chewing her cud, sometimes turning to gaze out of liquid brown eyes, without astonishment, at the small human being at her side. In return Mabel spent hours at a time whisking flies off the cow with a green branch. She spent hours, too – more arduous ones – pumping and carrying pails of water to fill Daisy's trough. It was quite a trick to make the water come – first by using short strokes in rapid succession, then by pulling the long pump handle slowly up and down. She could not carry a full pail, of course, and this meant that she had to make many trips before the trough was full. It was sad that after this effort Daisy always refused to come and drink right away, and would only do it in her own good time. But she had her moments of affection, when she followed Mabel wherever she went, even to the point of getting stuck between two hedges on a narrow path and standing there for ages, placidly chewing her cud, refusing to back up. They were both contrary characters, the little girl and the cow, but they respected each other.

In my mind's eye I see my mother running through those two years (how fleet her step even when she was in her seventies!) – across dappled light and shadow, always green leaves over her head and sunlight splashing down, alone with the cries of birds and the swift, shallow river. She wrote, 'It was as if my mind and heart had been tied up with hundreds of careful strings and these were suddenly loosened and fell away. O marvel, O inexhaustible dream, O happiness!'

But solitude is one thing and loneliness is another. She was at times cruelly lonely. The two women used, for instance, to go out at night to play cards with the neighbours some distance away, leaving the little girl to suffer such agonies of fear as only those who have experienced them can imagine, while she sat shivering in the dark at the top of the stairs, quaking at the hoot of an owl or the creak of a branch, until at last – sometimes as late as midnight – the footsteps on the path meant that she was saved. Grannie, it is true, 'grew fond' of her 'in the end' and could be 'trusted'. How fearful to remember that Aunt Mollie could not – this presence fearsome in its reserve and strangeness, like some goddess who could not be placated. It was Aunt Mollie who looked coldly at the child one day and said, 'You have a mean little mouth,' inflicting one of those wounds that rise up to haunt a lifetime; my mother winced visibly each time she remembered it, as if she really wondered to the end if it were true, as if she had been marked by it, and some childlike sense of herself as the beautiful being she was had been poisoned there and then, forever. Aunt Mollie was the creature of moods, sometimes humming and singing all day, then suddenly sullen, with a sullenness that might break out any moment into violence when she moved about the house exactly like a thunderstorm, banging the doors, and filling every corner with her darkness. At such times, sensible people kept out of her way. As a matter of fact, those angry fits interested Mabel very much, for she had had tantrums herself, and knew how difficult it was to control them. She remembered how her father had taken her on his knees during her outbursts and tried to help her. He had taught her to go off by herself at such times and hammer out her rage against a piece of wood with a hammer, or break sticks, letting the seizure play itself out against inanimate objects. So now on the dangerous days at the farm Mabel watched warily, and kept silent, or conferred with Daisy, or took long aerial rides in the orchard, where a swing had been set up for her and she could imagine she was flying.

No doubt Gervase Elwes's vision of the farm in Wales had included good country meals, fresh eggs and milk. The reality was rather different. Eggs were a rarity – most of them went to market – and those custards dear to English hearts were fabricated with something called Canary custard powder. On Sunday evenings, the three at the farm had a small glass of fresh milk each, as a special treat, for the milk, too, had to be sold for cash. But there were compensations. My mother always remembered and spoke of the breakfast bacon, which was broiled in long strips that hung from a tin contraption set upon the live coals of the grate. It tasted delicious. Sometimes there were also mushrooms, collected before breakfast in the dewy grass. The child's great unsatisfied craving was for sweet things. Sugar was kept locked up in a glass-doored cupboard, so she got into the habit of sneaking into the kitchen, getting up on a chair, and dipping a finger into a can of sweet condensed milk that was kept on the top of the stove, then greedily sucking off the sweetness.

One day, Aunt Mollie came in as she was at this stolen pleasure. Aunt Mollie was in one of her fits.

She yanked the child down by the hair and shook her violently. Then, as the paroxysm rose to its climax, she banged the can down on the table and forced the child's face on it, again and again, till her mouth and cheeks were badly cut and scratched by the sharp tin edges. 'I'll teach you, you thieving little brat!' It took Grannie's sharp command – the one word 'Moll!' – to break the terrifying atmosphere of uncontrolled rage. The possessed woman pushed the child away, laid her head on the table, and gave way to long, retching sobs. Mabel, too frightened to cry yet, just stood there, licking the scratches around her mouth, while the old woman went over to her daughter, laid a hand on her shoulder, and said, 'Moll, my poor Moll, what have you done now?'

Mabel had been too shocked to feel pain, but then the scratches began to hurt rather badly and she cried out in her distress. At last, Grannie led her away, washed her face gently in warm water, and then sat for a long time in the parlour with the little girl in her lap, rocking the grief away and leaning her head now and then on the curly one, as if to rest a burden there. At this point, Mabel began to enjoy the drama of the situation and to long to talk about it. She felt that she had some experience of such matters, and wanted to explain about the hammer and sticks. The old woman smiled down into the earnest face rather sadly but said nothing, and just rolled the child up in a blanket and left her on the sofa to have a nap – left her feeling a little jealous, for it was clear that Grannie's thoughts were elsewhere.

Somehow or other, this scene cleared away some of the resentment that had no doubt been building up in Aunt Mollie since the intruder arrived. For quite some time afterward, she was gentle, once even touching Mabel's face with a tentative finger, as if to ask whether the scratches still hurt. There was a change in Grannie, too. She found little ways of showing the child affection – a piece of sugar hidden in Mabel's apron pocket, or a glass of real milk by her bed at night. It seemed almost as if all would be well.

At this time, Mabel was entirely absorbed in a new companion, a bedraggled, starving kitten that she had found one day on her rambles and brought home to care for and feed. It was a miserable sight at first, so dirty that one could not tell what colour it might be, but it soon licked itself clean and emerged a tiny tabby with every stripe in place. Aunt Mollie disapproved strongly of the whole affair. But Grannie said the child could keep the cat, provided she trained it herself and cleaned up after it meanwhile. At last, the little girl had something on which to lavish affection, something that responded, something her own.

Then, one unlucky day when they were all away for some time and the kitten was left locked up alone too long in the house, it chose Aunt Mollie's room to be dirty in. When they came back, Mabel's first thought was for her kitten, but while she was still looking around for it downstairs, she heard a scream from upstairs, a sound of running feet, and then a high, mounting cry of distress from the kitten as it flew through the air and fell at the bottom of the stairs with a soft thud. Aunt Mollie got there before the child could, caught the kitten up as it tried to crawl away, and, holding it by the nape of the neck, made as if to beat it against the wall. Mabel, suddenly beside herself with rage, flung herself at Aunt Mollie like a wild animal, biting and kicking and screaming, 'I'll kill you!'

They did not see Grannie, but, clasped together in fury as they were, they felt her there, standing silent at the door, as the kitten crawled off and hid under the cupboard. Locked in that strange embrace, they turned, frozen by the presence of the quiet old woman. She still said nothing, only leaned her head against one hand on the frame of the door. Then she gave each of them in turn a long, piercing look that, my mother wrote, 'made me feel older and Aunt Mollie seem childish'. There was no scolding. Mabel was sent upstairs to clean up in Aunt Mollie's room. The old woman turned to her daughter gravely: 'Moll, I have to talk to you . . .'

How dreadfully quiet a house in which violence has taken place seems when it is over. Upstairs in her attic room, the child waited. Finally, Grannie came, bearing a glass of milk and a piece of cake on a tray; there was another glass on the tray, for by this time Aunt Mollie had also been sent to bed. 'The kitten is all right. One leg bruised, that's all. No bones broken.'

Hours later, Mabel woke, feeling certain that she had heard a door open and the stairs creak. She sat bolt upright, listening, then crept out to discover that in fact Aunt Mollie's door was open. Panic seized her. Had Aunt Mollie gone after the kitten again? The child stole down the stairs on bare feet, guided by a faint light from the kitchen. There was no sound. She crept along the hall until she could see through the crack of the half-open door. What she saw was the woman kneeling beside the kitten's basket, holding a small saucepan of milk to warm over a candle on the floor beside her, her empty glass nearby. Her face was blotched from crying and looked inexpressibly forlorn and wretched. After a very long time of this tense silence, the milk seemed warm enough to be poured out into a saucer. The kitten meanwhile was sitting up in the basket, watching all this as intently as Mabel did. But it did not move when Aunt Mollie held the saucer out, whispering, 'Come, kitten, come.' The kitten was sleepy, and Aunt Mollie was not good at cajoling. (Would she get impatient? Mabel wondered with terror.) At last, it made up its mind, stretched stiffly as it came out of the basket, shaking the bruised leg as if to unkink it, and settled down peacefully to lap the warm milk. Aunt Mollie reached out one finger to stroke its back, very gently. At this point, it was all Mabel could do not to cry out, 'They don't like to be touched while they are eating!' Indeed, the kitten stopped lapping, withdrew a little, twitched its fur where the finger had touched it, and then – Oh, relief! – went back to the saucer again. Mabel crept back to bed full of bewilderment and a painful wonder.

A few days later, Grannie told the child that a doctor was coming to see Aunt Mollie, and that Mabel was to play out of doors and keep out of the way while he was there. The little girl went down to the swing in the orchard, and swayed slowly back and forth, chanting songs she had made up. She was called out of this dreamy state of contentment by Grannie's voice, shrill and anxious, asking her to come right away; the doctor wished to talk to her. 'What does he want?' Mabel asked fearfully, as she walked toward the house at Grannie's side. 'I'm not ill.'

'Tell the truth, child,' the old woman said sternly. 'That's what he wants.'

It was all rather solemn, taking place in the parlour, a room always dim because the geraniums in the window shut out most of the light. The doctor was sitting there, a large, fat man dressed in black, his knees spread wide and, between them, a small table with papers laid out upon it. He looked out at the three with a hard suspicious look, and Mabel took an instant dislike to him, comparing him in her written account to a piece of cold fat on the edge of her plate, which it made her quite sick just to imagine. 'Stand here,' he commanded, pointing to a place just in front of him, as if she were a criminal. He asked her name and age, and wrote them down. He asked her how long she had lived there – but how could she answer this? There had been no time in Wales; it was forever and a day. Grannie, after some calculating, answered for her, 'Seven months'. This voice from the other side of the room caught the child's attention, and she turned to look at the two women, sitting there, at either end of the black horse-hair sofa. Aunt Mollie was gazing steadily over the man's bald head at the geraniums in the window. She was behaving as if he did not exist.

In the story as my mother wrote it, it is not clear whether this doctor was an official personage, sent for, perhaps, at the request of a neighbour, or whether the old woman herself had sent for him, torn between responsibility for her small charge and for her troubling, troubled daughter, and hoping to have a terrible decision taken out of her hands. Whatever Grannie had had in mind, it is clear that by the time the doctor arrived, he was not welcome. That grave command, 'Tell the truth', laid a heavy burden on a seven year old; in fact, Grannie was putting the decision up to the child.

The doctor rapped out the next question with a knock of his glasses on the table: 'Are you happy here?'

'Of course I am,' Mabel answered crossly. She felt a very contrary mood coming on.

'And are you never afraid of your Aunt Mollie?'

'No, never,' Mabel said, without a second's hesitation. She did more; she went over to the sofa, sat down beside Aunt Mollie, and slipped a hand under the woman's arm and down into her hands, folded in her lap – a gesture so extraordinary that it could only have been called out by extraordinary circumstances. But the child sensed that he was trying to get her to take sides against Grannie and Aunt Mollie, and, whatever happened, she was on their side. So there they sat, the three of them lined up on the sofa, and he, the enemy, watching them. Deprived of whatever dreadful secret he had come to ferret out, the doctor snapped his spectacles into their hard, shiny case and got up to go. Grannie escorted him stiffly and politely to the door, and in the second when their backs were turned, Aunt Mollie glanced at Mabel, and the child saw something like a twinkle come and go in those blue eyes, in an instant's humorous exchange of triumph. Was it a recognition of loyalty, perhaps? Or perhaps, at long last, love? Never again did the woman hurt the child, although she still had stormy door-banging days.

How often we talked, my mother and I, of going back to Wales someday and finding the little valley, the lonely farm, the orchard, the swift, shallow river

– even, perhaps, the hazel hedge where Mabel and her brother, when he was there for the holidays, had once cut out a secret hiding place. We never did. But perhaps such vivid memories need no renewal in time. They are there, curled up like Japanese flowers; one has only to dip them into the waters of consciousness for them to open and fill the heart. So it was for me when the story of what really happened in Wales was superimposed upon the glimpses I had had of that time as a child. Some of the sheen went, as I read through those pages in my mother's hand, which tell in detail all that I have written here, and something harder and deeper took its place. Now, thinking of my mother as she was when I knew her – of her compassion and of the fire that blazed up in her whenever injustice was done, of the startling and wholly unsentimental truth of her perceptions – I think of the little girl in Wales who learned so much through such unconventional means. It was not dreadful or wrong at all, what happened to her there, but a time full of secret riches, which she understood because she was already the person she was to become, able to face reality, and to face it with complete courage, on her own terms.

From *I Knew a Phoenix*, published by The Women's Press.

A LETTER FROM GEORGE SAND TO HER MOTHER, SOPHIE

31 May 1831

My Dear Maman,

You are not feeling very cheerful, are you, because you are still going to be alone. Congenial companionship is very difficult to combine with liberty. You like to have people with you, but you hate any kind of constraint, and that is just like me. How is one to reconcile one's own desires with other people's? I really don't know. Perhaps one really ought to shut one's eyes to a great many little things, to tolerate a great many imperfections in human nature and to resign oneself to certain annoyances which are inevitable whatever one's circumstances may be. Are you not rather severe towards transient wrong-doing? It is true that you forgive easily and forget quickly; but are you not a little hasty in condemnation? For me, my dear, liberty of thought and action is the first of blessings. If one could combine with that the little cares of bringing up a family it would be much sweeter, but is that at all possible? The one is always a nuisance to the other, liberty to one's home-circle, and one's home-circle to liberty! You are the only judge in the question of which you would prefer to sacrifice! I know that my own greatest fault lies in the fact that I *cannot* submit to the least shadow of constraint. Everything that is imposed on me as a duty becomes odious at once; whatever I do of my own free will is done with all my heart. It is often a great misfortune to be made like that and all my failings towards other people when they do occur, originate there.

But can one change one's own nature? If people are very indulgent to this fault of mine I find that it corrects itself in the most wonderful way. But when I am perpetually reproached about it, it gets much worse, and really that is not out of a spirit of contradiction; it is just involuntary, irresistible! I really must venture to tell you, dear Maman, that you have very little idea what I am really like. It is a long time now since we lived together and you often forget that I am now twenty-seven years old and that my character was bound to undergo many changes since I was quite a girl.

You seem to impute a love of pleasure and a need of frivolous amusement to me that I am far from possessing. It is not society, and noise, and theatres and new dresses that I want; you are the only person to make that mistake, it is liberty that I long for. I want to be able to walk out quite alone and say to myself: 'I will dine at four, or at seven, just as I like. I will go to the Tuileries through the Luxembourg instead of the Champs Elysées if the whim seizes me.' That would please me far better than the ordinariness of ordinary people and the stiffness of drawing-rooms.

If I meet people who are dense enough to take my innocent fantasies for hypocritical vices I cannot persuade myself to take the trouble to undeceive them. I only know that such people bore me, misunderstand me ... yes ... and outrage me! I make no answer. As far as I am concerned they are wiped out. Is there anything to blame in that? I seek neither vengeance nor reparation for I am not vindictive: I simply forget. I know people say I am not a serious person because there is no hatred in me and I have not the pride to justify myself.

Oh, God! What is this frantic desire to torment each other, which possesses human beings? This frantic desire to reprove each other's faults bitterly, to condemn pitilessly, everyone who is not cut upon our own pattern.

You, dear Maman, have suffered much from the intolerance and false virtues of high-principled people. How terribly at one time they blackened your beauty, your youth, your independence, your happy facile character? What bitterness poisoned your brilliant destiny! If you had had a tender indulgent mother who opened her arms to you at each fresh sorrow and said to you, 'Men may condemn you, but I absolve you! Let them curse ... for I bless you!', what a comfort it would have been to you in all that disgustingness and littleness of life!

So someone has been telling you *that it is I who wear the breeches*. It is not a bit true, if you were to be here for twenty-four hours, you would see that it was not. On the other hand I have not the slightest desire to see my husband in petticoats. Let us each wear our own clothes and be equally free. I have my faults, but my husband has his, and if I were to tell you that ours is a model household and that there is never a cloud between us you would not believe me. There is good and bad in my circumstances, just as there is for everyone else. The fact is that my husband does just as he likes. He has mistresses or does not have them, as his appetite dictates to him; he drinks muscat grape juice or plain water according to his desire at the moment; he saves or spends just as he feels inclined; he builds, plants, makes changes, and rules the property and the house just as he intends. I have not a word to say in any of it.

I don't mind because I know he is a good organiser, that he is more inclined to be economical than to waste money and that he loves his children, and looks at everything from the point of view of their welfare. As you may see, I have no feelings for him but esteem and confidence and since I have given the property entirely into his control, I suppose no one will continue to suspect me of wishing to dominate him.

I need so little, nothing but the same income and the same standard of comfort that you have. I should be satisfied with an allowance of three thousand francs a year, considering that I can already add to it with my pen. For the rest, it is only fair that my husband's absolute liberty should be reciprocal; if that were not the case he would become hateful and contemptible to me, and that he does not wish! I therefore live quite independently. I go to bed when he thinks it is time to get up. I can start off to La Châtre if I like, or just as easily to Rome; I come in at midnight, or at six in the morning. It is entirely my own business. Please judge anyone who criticises me for it with the head and the heart of a mother, for both ought to be on my side.

I shall go to Paris this summer. The more you show me that I am dear to you and that you are pleased to have me with you, the happier and the more grateful you will find me. But if I find bitter criticism and offensive suspicion in your orbit (it is not from you that I fear them) I will make room for the more powerful, and without vengeance, without anger, I will enjoy the peace of my own conscience and my liberty. You really have too much mind and heart not to realise soon that I do not deserve all this hard treatment.

Good-bye dear little Maman. My children are well. Solange is lovely and naughty. Maurice is too thin really, but such a good boy. I am so pleased with his character and his mental development. I rather spoil my fat little girl. But the fact that Maurice has become so sweet now reassures me for their future.

Write soon, dear Maman,
Kisses with all my soul.

From *Between Ourselves: Letters Between Mothers and Daughters 1750–1982*, edited by Karen Payne, published by Michael Joseph/Virago Press.

A LETTER FROM SYLVIA PLATH
TO HER MOTHER, AURELIA

23 April 1956

Dear Mother,

Well, finally the blundering American Express sent me your letter from Rome . . . our minds certainly work on the same track!

. . . I have already planned to stay in London three nights and have written to reserve a room for us; we'll just eat and talk the day you come, but for the next two I'll get some theatre tickets and we'll plan jaunts to flowering parks, Piccadilly, Trafalgar Square . . . walking, strolling, feeding pigeons and sunning ourselves like happy clams. Then, to Cambridge, where I have already reserved a room for you for two nights . . . I have made a contract with one of my husky men to teach me how to manage a punt before you come, so you shall step one afternoon from your room at the beautiful Garden House Hotel right on to the [River] Cam and be boated up to Granchester through weeping willows for tea in an orchard! Worry about nothing. Just let me know your predilections and it shall be accomplished . . .

You, alone, of all, have had crosses that would cause many a stronger woman to break under the never-ceasing load. You have borne daddy's long, hard death and taken on a man's portion in your work; you have fought your own ulcer attacks, kept us children sheltered, happy, rich with art and music lessons, camp and play; you have seen me through that black night when the only word I knew was No and when I thought I could never write or think again; and, you have been brave through your own operation. Now, just as you begin to breathe, this terrible slow, dragging pain comes upon you, almost as if it would be too easy to free you so soon from the deepest, most exhausting care and giving of love.

. . . Know with a certain knowing that *you* deserve, too, to be with the loved ones who can give you strength in your trouble: Warren and myself. Think of your trip here as a trip to the heart of strength in your daughter who loves you more dearly than words can say. I am waiting for you, and your trip shall be for your own soul's health and growing. You need . . . a context where all burdens are not on your shoulders, where some loving person comes to heft the hardest, to walk beside you. Know this, and know that it is right you should come. You need to imbibe power and health and serenity to return to your job . . .

I feel with all my joy and life that these are qualities I can give you, from the fullness and brimming of my heart. So come, and slowly we will walk through green gardens and marvel at this strange and sweet world.

Your own loving sivvy

From *Letters Home*, edited by Aurelia S Plath, published by Faber and Faber.

FROM *THE SCARLET THREAD –* *AS TOLD TO RACHEL BARTON –* *AN INDIAN WOMAN SPEAKS*

It is time I told you about my family. My father and mother were both of the tailoring caste. This is a middling sort of caste with some above us and some below. As you probably know we usually have to marry within the caste, and this is true even in Britain. I believe this custom is dying out amongst some educated people. My parents had ten children, but three died young. The ones who lived were my eldest brother Krishna, my second brother Veejay, and the girls, Sheelah the eldest, then Indira, Prem and Asha in order, with me Sita the youngest girl. When they were first married, my parents were quite well off, but by the time I was born they were poor; I will explain why later. So my mother had to work as well as my father, but because she had been respected in the village she never worked there but preferred to go every day to surrounding villages, sometimes as far as six or seven miles away. Every day she would walk there and back with her sewing machine on her shoulder, unless there was a wedding or other special occasion when she would stay the night. It would have been dangerous for her to walk back alone in the dark as there were sometimes bad men about who might have attacked her. She was popular with the farmers and their wives for whom she worked, so at these feasts they would give her plenty of food to take home, enough for several days.

I have never heard of any other mother who did so much for her family and loved them all so well. When she was not sewing for other families she would sew for us, making clothes and everything we needed in the house. I never saw her idle, for she would cook and clean and milk the animals and look after the garden. I always wanted to be near her and would sleep near her wherever she was. While she was away I longed for her, sometimes so much that when my sisters or brothers were angry with me I would run out of the house and look for her in the villages, sometimes running for miles. Mother meant everything to us and she took responsibility for everything. As she could not be with us very much she was very firm, even stern, and we were frightened to offend her. We did not resent this for we knew she loved us and wanted our good.

I often wondered how Mother could live with so little sleep. She only lay down on her bed when she was ill, and this did not often happen. Then she would refuse to see a doctor or take any medicine; in spite of this she always recovered quite soon. In the evening when others were resting after a day's work she would sit cross-legged on the floor on her blanket in front of her sewing machine, the light bulb pulled down low over her head so that she could see to work. During the night she would doze off from time to time and her head would drop forward, but she would wake with a jerk and go on sewing. Less often she would sink down on to her blanket and sleep a little. I know just how it was because as usual I slept close to her.

Often there were three or four girls from our street – one rich girl, a friend of Asha's, my next elder sister, and sometimes more girls from around – who would come to spend the evening and perhaps bring their quilts and stay the night. It was Mother who attracted them because she was lively and friendly and stayed up so late while their mothers went early to bed. The girls would bring their books to study when exams were near. Mother would say to them, 'Read aloud to me, then I will know you are really studying.' She would listen as she sewed and one girl after another read from her book.

Sometimes about midnight we would make tea to refresh ourselves. It was like having a night party and I loved it. If we had no tea or milk I would go with the girls to a neighbour's house and knock on the door to wake them up and shout, 'Open up the shop, we need tea and milk.' Sometimes they would curse and grumble, but we would say, 'Please help us, we have exams tomorrow.' This would make them sorry for us, so someone would take a lantern and go to the shop to sell us the tea and milk. If no one would help us we would do without and boil up some fennel leaves instead. How often later I was to remember those happy times and wonder if girls in the village were still the same.

* * *

At the age of fifteen, Sita entered into an arranged marriage with Nirmal and was brought to London to live in her mother-in-law's household. It wasn't long before Nirmal started beating her.

* * *

I can't remember why Nirmal started to beat me that day; it went on and on until I was almost out of my mind. I longed to escape even to death. 'I'm going for ever,' I cried, 'I'll kill myself rather than live like this.' Hearing me shout, Nimmo came into the room. I ran to the front door and as I opened it Nirmal shouted, 'All right, do as you please.' I heard Nimmo echo his words as he caught hold of me and threw me outside. As I picked myself up I heard the door being locked behind me. I ran into the street and there I saw Anuz coming towards me as he left the pub on the corner of the street. 'What has happened?' he cried. 'I heard screams coming from our place.'

'Your brother has been battering me, that is why; and now I'm going to kill myself.'

'Go then,' he answered, and slapped my face.

I could think of nothing but escape from pain and hopelessness. Even my children were for that moment forgotten. The Underground was not far away, so I ran there and started down the stairs. Suddenly I came face to face with a group of women I knew. They were going home from the factory after work. They looked at me in astonishment and crowded around me. 'What are you doing here, running round with your clothes all torn and your feet bare?' I tried to pass them but they held me and started to drag me back. I was by then crying and screaming. If they had not been there and stopped me I know I should have thrown myself in front of the first train, without hesitation and without regret.

The women were shocked and distressed to see me in this state but when they took me back to the flat they dared not say too much as their boss was a friend of Anuz. Anuz and Nimmo and Nirmal may have felt some fear that they would be blamed and looked put out when the women brought me back. They said nothing to me and I went to my room and lay down on the bed exhausted. I cried until I fell asleep for a while. When I woke up I felt numb and unreal. I got up and went into the kitchen. The washing up had been left undone, so I washed the dishes and made some chapatis as if nothing had happened. No one mentioned it again, but the memory of that evening comes back to me time after time.

Meanwhile in India my mother was hearing about what had happened to me as people from our village returned on holiday or came back to stay. Although it is not unusual for girls to be ill-treated when they marry, very few are battered as I was, and you can imagine what misery and guilt my mother felt. She wondered what she could do to help me, but without money she was powerless. Then Asha wrote to her from Leicester asking if she would come over and look after her two little children so that she could go back to work. Asha said she would send over the fare, so Mother made immediate arrangements to come. It was not difficult to get permission. When Asha wrote and told me that Mother was coming I could hardly believe it; I had longed for her so often, and our letters had meant very little. This was because I had never told her the truth about my life.

Mother's fare was paid for to Leicester but she only stayed there for one day. She asked Asha for the fare to London, where she could stay with Indira, and planned to see me as soon as possible. I told Nirmal that she was coming, and as usual he forbade me to go to Indira's place to meet her. I did not care if he killed me as long as I saw Mother! He went out and I put the two children in the old pram and made the long journey to her house. I saw Mother standing at the door looking out for me, and she looked just the same. I had forgotten that I did not, and when she saw me Mother nearly fainted. She leaned against the door and started to cry. I put my arms around her and kept saying, 'I'm all right, Mother.' She hugged me and said that she could hardly recognise me, I was so thin and ill. She was so concerned for me she scarcely noticed the two boys; in fact, as they were Nirmal's children she even felt she could not love them then. We went in and Indira gave us our dinner. I had only seen her occasionally, as Nirmal had quarrelled violently with her husband long ago and he did not welcome me in the house.

Mother and I talked and talked, there was so much to go over. She told me that she was going to take me away, but I did not really think it possible. 'You must think I have a heart of stone', she said, 'to send my poor daughters so far away to take their chance in a strange land, but I did not know. You will not suffer any more.' I told her I must go back home or Nirmal would beat me again and asked her to come with me. Indira wanted her to stay, but Mother said she would go to protect me. 'Who else ever tried to protect you? Nobody,' she said. So we went home, and as Nirmal was late we had time to make plans. Mother told me to go and look for all my documents, my passport, marriage certificate, and the children's birth certificates. I went through Nirmal's papers and found them. Then she told me to pack a few things for myself and the children, but to say nothing to him. He came back very late and Mother had gone into the bedroom to rest. She heard him shout and abuse me and I thought she might come in and protect me, but when she did she was very polite to Nirmal, even flattering, and I realised that she was a clever woman. He started to confide in her, telling her that he was short of money and had bills he could not pay. She was sympathetic and said, 'I will take Sita and the children back to Leicester with me for a few days. We will stay with Asha and you will be able to save some money for your bills. I will pay the fares for them.' Nirmal was pleased to think he would have us out of the way for a while and bit more money to drink and gamble with. He agreed and even went to bed in a better temper than usual. He thought my mother approved of him!

Next morning I got ready to go, terrified that Nirmal would find I had taken the papers. He came with us to the station, but irritable as he often was in the morning he found fault with me. 'What do you think you look like, stupid thing, in those dreadful old clothes? You should be ashamed.' He began to kick me in front of everyone on the platform. Still my mother said nothing, though she told me afterwards that her hands were clenched so hard that they pained her. We got into the train and Nirmal stood outside by the half-open window. Just before the train started,

Mother came to the window and spoke to him in a loud clear voice. 'You will never see even the shadow of my daughter again.' I thought with terror that he would jump on the train and pull me out on to the platform, but he stood there without moving, too astonished to do anything. The train started, he turned away and I hoped I would be free of him for ever. My wonderful mother had saved my life. Now a new life would begin for me and my children.

From *The Scarlet Thread – As Told to Rachel Barton – An Indian Woman Speaks*, published by Virago Press.

VIRGINIA WOOLF
from
MOMENTS OF BEING

Until I was in the forties – I could settle the date by
seeing when I wrote *To the Lighthouse*, but am too
casual here to bother to do it – the presence of my
mother obsessed me. I could hear her voice, see her,
imagine what she would do or say as I went about
my day's doings. She was one of the invisible presences who after all play so important a part in every
life. This influence, by which I mean the consciousness of other groups impinging upon ourselves;
public opinion; what other people say and think; all
those magnets which attract us this way to be like
that, or repel us the other and make us different
from that; has never been analysed in any of those
Lives which I so much enjoy reading, or very super-
ficially.

Yet it is by such invisible presences that the 'subject
of this memoir' is tugged this way and that every

day of his life; it is they that keep him in position. Consider what immense forces society brings to play upon each of us, how that society changes from decade to decade; and also from class to class; well, if we cannot analyse these invisible presences, we know very little of the subject of the memoir; and again how futile life-writing becomes. I see myself as a fish in a stream; deflected; held in place; but cannot describe the stream.

To return to the particular instance which should be more definite and more capable of description than for example the influence on me of the Cambridge Apostles, or the influence of the Galsworthy, Bennett, Wells school of fiction, or the influence of the Vote, or of the War – that is, the influence of my mother. It is perfectly true that she obsessed me, in spite of the fact that she died when I was thirteen, until I was forty-four. Then one day walking round Tavistock Square I made up, as I sometimes make up my books, *To the Lighthouse*; in a great, apparently involuntary, rush. One thing burst into another. Blowing bubbles out of a pipe gives the feeling of the rapid crowd of ideas and scenes which blew out of my mind, so that my lips seemed syllabling of their own accord as I walked. What blew the bubbles? Why then? I have no notion. But I wrote the book very quickly; and when it was written, I ceased to be obsessed by my mother. I no longer hear her voice; I do not see her.

I suppose that I did for myself what psychoanalysts do for their patients. I expressed some very long felt and deeply felt emotion. And in expressing it I explained it and then laid it to rest. But what is the meaning of 'explained' it? Why, because I described

her and my feeling for her in that book, should my
vision of her and my feeling for her become so much
dimmer and weaker? Perhaps one of these days I shall
hit on the reason; and if so, I will give it, but at the
moment I will go on, describing what I can remember, for it may be true that what I remember of her
now will weaken still further. (This note is made
provisionally, in order to explain in part why it is
now so difficult to give any clear description of her.)

Certainly there she was, in the very centre of that
great Cathedral space which was childhood; there she
was from the very first. My first memory is of her
lap; the scratch of some beads on her dress comes
back to me as I pressed my cheek against it. Then I
see her in her white dressing gown on the balcony;
and the passion flower with the purple star on its
petals. Her voice is still faintly in my ears – decided,
quick; and in particular the little drops with which
her laugh ended – three diminishing ahs . . . 'Ah –
ah – ah . . .' I sometimes end a laugh that way myself.
And I see her hands, like Adrian's, with the very
individual square-tipped fingers, each finger with a
waist to it, and the nail broadening out. (My own
are the same size all the way, so that I can slip a ring
over my thumb.) She had three rings; a diamond
ring, an emerald ring, and an opal ring. My eyes
used to fix themselves upon the lights in the opal as
it moved across the page of the lesson book when
she taught us, and I was glad that she left it to me (I
gave it to Leonard). Also I hear the tinkle of her
bracelets, made of twisted silver, given her by Mr
Lowell, as she went about the house; especially as she
came up at night to see if we were asleep, holding a
candle shaded; this is a distinct memory, for, like all

children, I lay awake sometimes and longed for her to come. Then she told me to think of all the lovely things I could imagine. Rainbows and bells . . . But besides these minute separate details, how did I first become conscious of what was always there − her astonishing beauty? Perhaps I never became conscious of it; I think I accepted her beauty as the natural quality that a mother − she seemed typical, universal, yet our own in particular − had by virtue of being our mother. It was part of her calling. I do not think that I separated her face from that general being; or from her whole body. Certainly I have a vision of her now, as she came up the path by the lawn at St Ives; slight, shapely − she held herself very straight. I was playing. I stopped, about to speak to her. But she half turned from us, and lowered her eyes. From that indescribably sad gesture I knew that Philips, the man who had been crushed on the line and whom she had been visiting, was dead. It's over, she seemed to say. I knew, and was awed by the thought of death. At the same time I felt that her gesture as a whole was lovely. Very early, through nurses or casual visitors, I must have known that she was thought very beautiful. But that pride was snobbish, not a pure and private feeling: it was mixed with pride in other people's admiration. It was related to the more definitely snobbish pride caused in me by the nurses who said one night talking together while we ate our supper: 'They're very well connected . . .'

But apart from her beauty, if the two can be separated, what was she herself like? Very quick; very direct; practical; and amusing, I say at once offhand. She could be sharp, she disliked affectation. 'If you put your head on one side like that, you shan't come to the party,' I remember she said to me as we drew up in a carriage in front of some house. Severe; with a background of knowledge that made her sad. She had her own sorrow waiting behind her to dip into privately. Once when she had set us to write exercises I looked up from mine and watched her reading – the Bible perhaps; and, struck by the gravity of her face, told myself that her first husband had been a clergyman and that she was thinking, as she read what he had read, of him. This was a fable on my part; but it shows that she looked very sad when she was not talking.

But can I get any closer to her without drawing upon all those descriptions and anecdotes which after she was dead imposed themselves upon my view of her? Very quick; very definite; very upright; and behind the active, the sad, the silent. And of course she was central. I suspect the word 'central' gets closest to the general feeling I had of living so completely in her atmosphere that one never got far enough away from her to see her as a person. (That is one reason why I see the Gibbses and the Beadles and the Clarkes so much more distinctly.) She was the whole thing; Talland House was full of her; Hyde Park Gate was full of her. I see now, though the sentence is hasty, feeble and inexpressive, why it was that it was impossible for her to leave a very private and particular impression upon a child. She was keeping what I call in my shorthand the panoply of life – that which we all lived in common – in being. I see now that she was living on such an extended surface that she had not time, nor strength, to concentrate, except for a moment if one were ill or in some child's crisis, upon me, or upon anyone – unless it were Adrian. Him she cherished separately; she called him 'My Joy'. The later view, the understanding that I now have of her position must have its say; and it shows me that a woman of forty with seven children, some of them needing grown-up attention, and four still in the nursery; and an eighth, Laura, an idiot, yet living with us; and a husband fifteen years her elder, difficult, exacting, dependent on her; I see now that a woman who had to keep all this in being and under control must have been a general presence rather than a particular person to a child of seven or eight. Can I remember ever being alone with her for more than a few minutes? Someone was always interrupting. When I think of her spontaneously she is always in a room full of people; Stella, George and Gerald are there; my father, sitting reading with one leg curled round the other, twisting his lock of hair; 'Go and take the crumb out of his beard,' she whispers to me; and off I trot. There are visitors, young men like Jack Hills who is in love with Stella; many young men, Cambridge friends of George's and Gerald's; old men, sitting round the tea table talking – father's friends, Henry James, Symonds, (I see him peering up at me on the broad staircase at St Ives with his drawn yellow face and a tie made of a yellow cord with two plush balls on it); Stella's friends – the Lushingtons, the Stillmans; I see her at the head of the table underneath the engraving of Beatrice given her by an old governess and painted blue; I hear jokes; laughter; the clatter of voices; I am teased; I say something funny; she laughs; I am pleased; I blush furiously; she observes; someone laughs at Nessa for saying that Ida Milman is her bf; Mother says soothingly, tenderly, 'Best friend, that means.' I see her going to the town with her basket; and Arthur Davies goes with her; I see her knitting on the hall step while we play cricket; I see her stretching her arms out to Mrs Williams when the bailiffs took possession of their house and the Captain stood at the window bawling and shying jugs, basins, chamber pots on to the gravel – 'Come to us, Mrs Williams'; 'No, Mrs Stephen,' sobbed Mrs Williams, 'I will not leave my husband.' – I see her writing at her table in London and the silver candlesticks, and the high carved chair with the claws and the pink seat; and the three-cornered brass ink pot.

* * *

She was born, I think, in 1848; I think in India; the daughter of Dr Jackson and his half-French wife. Not very much education came her way. An old governess – was she Mademoiselle Rose? did she give her the picture of Beatrice that hung in the dining room at Talland House? – taught her French, which she spoke with a very good accent; and she could play the piano and was musical. I remember that she kept De Quincey's *Opium Eater* on her table, one of her favourite books; and for a birthday present she chose all the works of Scott which her father gave her in the first edition – some remain; others are lost. For Scott she had a passion. She had an instinctive, not a trained mind. But her instinct, for books at least, seems to me to have been strong, and I liked it, for she gave a jump, I remember, when reading *Hamlet* aloud to her I misread 'sliver' 'silver' – she jumped as my father jumped at a false quantity when we read Virgil with him. She was her mother's favourite daughter of the three; and as her mother was an invalid even as a child she was used to nursing; to waiting on a sick bed. They had a house at Well Walk during the Crimean War; for there was an anecdote about watching the soldiers drill on the Heath. But her beauty at once came to the fore, even as a little girl; for there was another anecdote – how she could never be sent out alone, but must have Mary with her, to protect her from admiring looks: to keep her unconscious of that beauty – and she was, my father said, very little conscious of it. It was due to this beauty, I suspect, that she had that training which was much more important than any she had from governesses – the training of life at Little Holland House. She was a great deal at Little Holland House as a child, partly, I imagine, because she was acceptable to the painters, and the Prinseps – Aunt Sara and Uncle Thoby must have been proud of her.

Little Holland House was her world then. But what was that world like? I think of it as a summer afternoon world. To my thinking Little Holland House is an old white country house, standing in a large garden. Long windows open on to the lawn. Through them comes a stream of ladies in crinolines and little straw hats; they are attended by gentlemen in peg-top trousers and whiskers. The date is round about 1860. It is a hot summer day. Tea tables with great bowls of strawberries and cream are scattered about the lawn. They are 'presided over' by some of the six lovely sisters; who do not wear crinolines, but are robed in splendid Venetian draperies; they sit enthroned, and talk with foreign emphatic gestures – my mother too gesticulated, throwing her hands out – to the eminent men (afterwards to be made fun of by Lytton); rulers of India, statesmen, poets, painters. My mother comes out of the window wearing that striped silk dress buttoned at the throat with a flowing skirt that appears in the photograph. She is of course 'a vision' as they used to say; and there she stands, silent, with her plate of strawberries and cream; or perhaps is told to take a party across the garden to Signior's studio. The sound of music also comes from those long low rooms where the great Watts pictures hang; Joachim playing the violin; also the sound of a voice reading poetry – Uncle Thoby would read his translations from the Persian poets. How easy it is to fill in the picture with set pieces that I have gathered from memoirs – to bring in Tennyson in his wide-awake; Watts in his smock frock; Ellen Terry dressed as a boy; Garibaldi in his red shirt – and Henry Taylor turned from him to my mother – 'the face of one fair girl was more to me' – so he says in a poem. But if I turn to my mother, how difficult it is to single her out as she really was; to imagine what she was thinking, to put a single sentence into her mouth! I dream; I make up pictures of a summer's afternoon.

From *Moments of Being*, published widely.

Virginia Woolf

from

TO THE LIGHTHOUSE

No, she thought, putting together some of the pictures he had cut out – a refrigerator, a mowing machine, a gentleman in evening dress – children never forget. For this reason, it was so important what one said, and what one did, and it was a relief when they went to bed. For now she need not think about anybody. She could be herself, by herself. And that was what now she often felt the need of – to think; well not even to think. To be silent; to be alone. All the being and the doing, expansive, glittering vocal, evaporated; and one shrunk, with a sense of solemnity, to being oneself, a wedge-shaped core of darkness, something invisible to others. Although she continued to knit, and sat upright, it was thus that she felt herself; and this self having shed its attachments was free for the strangest adventures. When life sank down for a moment, the range of experience seemed limitless. And to everybody there was always this sense of unlimited resources, she supposed; one after another, she, Lily, Augustus Carmichael, must feel, our apparitions, the things you know us by, are simply childish. Beneath it is all dark, it is all spreading, it is unfathomably deep; but now and again we rise to the surface and that is what you see us by. Her horizon seemed to her limitless. There were all the places she had not seen; the Indian plains; she felt herself pushing aside the thick leather curtain of a church in Rome. This core of darkness could go anywhere, for no one saw it. They could not stop it, she thought, exulting. There was freedom, there was peace, there was, most welcome of all, a summoning together, a resting on a platform of stability. Not as oneself did one find rest ever, in her experience (she accomplished here something dexterous with her needles), but as a wedge of darkness. Losing personality, one lost the fret, the hurry, the stir; and there rose to her lips always some exclamation of triumph over life when things came together in this peace, this rest, this eternity; and pausing there she looked out to meet that stroke of the Lighthouse, the long steady stroke, the last of the three, which was her stroke, for watching them in this mood always at this hour one could not help attaching oneself to one thing especially of the things one saw; and this thing, the long steady stroke, was her stroke. Often she found herself sitting and looking, sitting and looking, with her work in her hands until she became the thing she looked at – that light for example. And it would lift up on it some little phrase or other which had been lying in her mind like that – 'Children don't forget, children don't forget' – which she would repeat and begin adding to it, It will end, It will end, she said. It will come, it will come, when suddenly she added, We are in the hands of the Lord.

But instantly she was annoyed with herself for saying that. Who had said it? not she; she had been trapped into saying something she did not mean. She looked up over her knitting and met the third stroke and it seemed to her like her own eyes meeting her own eyes, searching as she alone could search into her mind and her heart, purifying out of existence that lie, any lie. She praised herself in praising the light, without vanity, for she was stern, she was searching, she was beautiful like that light. It was odd, she thought, how if one was alone, one leant to things, inanimate things; trees, streams, flowers; felt they expressed one; felt they became one; felt they knew one, in a sense were one; felt an irrational tenderness thus (she looked at that long steady light) as for oneself. There rose, and she looked and looked with her needles suspended, there curled up off the floor of the mind, rose from the lake of one's being, a mist, a bride to meet her lover.

What brought her to say that: 'We are in the hands of the Lord'? she wondered. The insincerity slipping in among the truths roused her, annoyed her. She returned to her knitting again. How could any Lord have made this world? she asked. With her mind she had always seized the fact that there is no reason, order, justice: but suffering, death, the poor. There was no treachery too base for the world to commit; she knew that. No happiness lasted; she knew that. She knitted with firm composure, slightly pursing her lips and, without being aware of it, so stiffened and composed the lines of her face in a habit of sterness that when her husband passed, though he was chuckling at the thought that Hume, the philosopher, grown enormously fat, had stuck in a bog, he could not help noting, as he passed, the sternness at the heart of her beauty. It saddened him, and her remoteness pained him, and he felt, as he passed, that he could not protect her, and, when he reached the hedge, he was sad. He could do nothing to help her. He must stand by and watch her. Indeed, the infernal truth was, he made things worse for her. He was irritable – he was touchy. He had lost his temper over the Lighthouse. He looked into the hedge, into its intricacy, its darkness.

Always, Mrs Ramsay felt, one helped oneself out of solitude reluctantly by laying hold of some little odd or end, some sound, some sight. She listened, but it was all very still; cricket was over; the children were in their baths; there was only the sound of the sea. She stopped knitting; she held the long reddish-brown stocking dangling in her hands a moment. She saw the light again. With some irony in her interrogation, for when one woke at all, one's relations changed, she looked at the steady light, the pitiless, the remorseless, which was so much her, yet so little her, which had her at its beck and call (she woke in the night and saw it bent across their bed, stroking the floor), but for all that she thought, watching it with fascination, hypnotised, as if it were stroking with its silver fingers some sealed vessel in her brain whose bursting would flood her with delight, she had known happiness, exquisite happiness, intense happiness, and it silvered the rough waves a little more brightly, as daylight faded, and the blue went out of the sea and it rolled in waves of pure lemon which curved and swelled and broke upon the beach and the ecstasy burst in her eyes and waves of pure delight raced over the floor of her mind and she felt, It is enough! It is enough!

He turned and saw her. Ah! She was lovely, lovelier now than ever he thought. But he could not speak to her. He could not interrupt her. He wanted urgently to speak to her now that James was gone and she was alone at last. But he resolved, no; he would not interrupt her. She was aloof from him now in her beauty, in her sadness. He would let her be, and he passed her without a word, though it hurt him that she should look so distant, and he could not reach her, he could do nothing to help her. And again he would have passed her without a word had she not, at that very moment, given him of her own free will what she knew he would never ask, and called to him and taken the green shawl off the picture frame, and gone to him. For he wished, she knew, to protect her.

From *To the Lighthouse*, published widely.

MAYA ANGELOU

from

I KNOW WHY THE
CAGED BIRD SINGS

'Thou shall not be dirty' and 'Thou shall not be impudent' were the two commandments of Grandmother Henderson upon which hung our total salvation.

Each night in the bitterest winter we were forced to wash faces, arms, necks, legs and feet before going to bed. She used to add, with a smirk that unprofane people can't control when venturing into profanity, 'And wash as far as possible, then wash possible.'

We would go to the well and wash in the ice-cold, clear water, grease our legs with the equally cold stiff Vaseline, then tiptoe into the house. We wiped the dust from our toes and settled down for schoolwork, cornbread, clabbered milk, prayers and bed, always in that order. Momma was famous for pulling the quilts off after we had fallen asleep to examine our feet. If they weren't clean enough for her, she took the switch (she kept one behind the bedroom door for emergencies) and woke up the offender with a few aptly placed burning reminders.

The area around the well at night was dark and slick, and boys told about how snakes love water, so that anyone who had to draw water at night and then stand there alone and wash knew that moccasins and rattlers, puff adders and boa constrictors were winding their way to the well and would arrive just as the person washing got soap in her eyes. But Momma convinced us that not only was cleanliness next to Godliness, dirtiness was the inventor of misery.

The impudent child was detested by God and a shame to its parents and could bring destruction to its house and line. All adults had to be addressed as Mister, Missus, Miss, Auntie, Cousin, Unk, Uncle, Buhbah, Sister, Brother and a thousand other appellations indicating familial relationship and the lowliness of the addressor.

Everyone I knew respected these customary laws, except for the powhitetrash children.

Some families of powhitetrash lived on Momma's farm land behind the school. Sometimes a gaggle of them came to the Store, filling the whole room, chasing out the air and even changing the well-known scents. The children crawled over the shelves and into the potato and onion bins, twanging all the time in their sharp voices like cigar-box guitars. They took liberties in my Store that I would never dare. Since Momma told us that the less you say to white-folks (or even powhitetrash) the better, Bailey and I would stand, solemn, quiet in the displaced air. But

if one of the playful apparitions got close to us, I
pinched it. Partly out of angry frustration and partly
because I didn't believe in its flesh reality.

They called my uncle by his first name and ordered
him around the Store. He, to my crying shame,
obeyed them in his limping dip-straight-dip fashion.

My grandmother, too, followed their orders,
except that she didn't seem to be servile because she
anticipated their needs.

'Here's sugar, Miz Potter, and here's baking
powder. You didn't buy soda last month, you'll probably be needing some.'

Momma always directed her statements to the
adults, but sometimes, Oh painful sometimes, the
grimy, snotty-nosed girls would answer her.

'Naw, Annie . . .' – to Momma? Who owned the
land they lived on? Who forgot more than they
would ever learn? If there was any justice in the
world, God should strike them dumb at once! – 'Just
give us some extry sody crackers, and some more
mackerel.'

At least they never looked in her face, or I never
caught them doing so. Nobody with a smidgen of
training, not even the worst roustabout, would look
right in a grown person's face. It meant the person
was trying to take the words out before they were
formed. The dirty little children didn't do that, but
they threw their orders around the Store like lashes
from a cat-o'-nine-tails.

When I was around ten years old, those scruffy
children caused me the most painful and confusing
experience I had ever had with my grandmother.

One summer morning, after I had swept the dirt
yard of leaves, spearmint-gum wrappers and Vienna-

sausage labels, I raked the yellow-red dirt, and made half-moons carefully, so that the design stood out clearly and mask-like. I put the rake behind the Store and came through the back of the house to find Grandmother on the front porch in her big, wide white apron. The apron was so stiff by virtue of the starch that it could have stood alone. Momma was admiring the yard, so I joined her. It truly looked like a flat redhead that had been raked with a big-toothed comb. Momma didn't say anything but I knew she liked it. She looked over towards the school principal's house and to the right at Mr McElroy's. She was hoping one of those community pillars would see the design before the day's business wiped it out. Then she looked upward to the school. My head had swung with hers, so at just about the same time we saw a troop of the powhitetrash kids marching over the hill and down by the side of the school.

I looked to Momma for direction. She did an excellent job of sagging from her waist down, but from the waist up she seemed to be pulling for the top of the oak tree across the road. Then she began to moan a hymn. Maybe not to moan, but the tune was so slow and the metre so strange that she could have been moaning. She didn't look at me again. When the children reached halfway down the hill, halfway to the Store, she said without turning, 'Sister, go on inside.'

I wanted to beg her, 'Momma, don't wait for them. Come on inside with me. If they come in the Store, you go to the bedroom and let me wait on them. They only frighten me if you're around. Alone I know how to handle them.' But of course I couldn't say anything, so I went in and stood behind the screen door.

Before the girls got to the porch I heard their laughter crackling and popping like pine logs in a cooking stove. I suppose my lifelong paranoia was born in those cold, molasses-slow minutes. They came finally to stand on the ground in front of Momma. At first they pretended seriousness. Then one of them wrapped her right arm in the crook of her left, pushed out her mouth and started to hum. I realised that she was aping my grandmother. Another said, 'Naw, Helen, you ain't standing like her. This here's it.' Then she lifted her chest, folded her arms and mocked that strange carriage that was Annie Henderson. Another laughed, 'Naw, you can't do it. Your mouth ain't pooched out enough. It's like this.'

I thought about the rifle behind the door, but I knew I'd never be able to hold it straight, and the .410, our sawn-off shotgun, which stayed loaded and was fired ever New Year's night, was locked in the trunk and Uncle Willie had the key on his chain. Through the fly-specked screen-door, I could see that the arms of Momma's apron jiggled from the vibrations of her humming. But her knees seemed to have locked as if they would never bend again.

She sang on. No louder than before, but no softer either. No slower or faster.

The dirt of the girls' cotton dresses continued on their legs, feet, arms and faces to make them all of a piece. Their greasy uncoloured hair hung down, uncombed, with a grim finality. I knelt to see them better, to remember them for all time. The tears that had slipped down my dress left unsurprising dark spots, and made the front yard blurry and even more unreal. The world had taken a deep breath and was having doubts about continuing to revolve.

The girls had tired of mocking Momma and turned to other means of agitation. One crossed her eyes, stuck her thumbs in both sides of her mouth and said, 'Look here, Annie.' Grandmother hummed on and the apron strings trembled. I wanted to throw a handful of black pepper in their faces, to throw lye on them, to scream that they were dirty, scummy peckerwoods, but I knew I was as clearly imprisoned behind the scene as the actors outside were confined to their roles.

One of the smaller girls did a kind of puppet dance while her fellow clowns laughed at her. But the tall one, who was almost a woman, said something very quietly, which I couldn't hear. They all moved backward from the porch, still watching Momma. For an awful second I thought they were going to throw a rock at Momma, who seemed (except for the apron strings) to have turned into stone herself. But the big girl turned her back, bent down and put her hands flat on the ground – she didn't pick up anything. She simply shifted her weight and did a hand stand.

Her dirty bare feet and long legs went straight for the sky. Her dress fell down around her shoulders, and she had on no drawers. The slick pubic hair made a brown triangle where her legs came together. She hung in the vacuum of that lifeless morning for only a few seconds, then wavered and tumbled. The other girls clapped her on the back and slapped their hands.

Momma changed her song to 'Bread of Heaven, bread of Heaven, feed me till I want no more.'

I found that I was praying too. How long could Momma hold out? What new indignity would they think of to subject her to? Would I be able to stay out of it? What would Momma really like me to do?

Then they were moving out of the yard, on their way to town. They bobbed their heads and shook their slack behinds and turned, one at a time:

"Bye, Annie."

"Bye, Annie."

"Bye, Annie."

Momma never turned her head or unfolded her arms, but she stopped singing and said, "Bye, Miz Helen, 'bye, Miz Ruth, 'bye, Miz Eloise."

I burst. A firecracker July-the-Fourth burst. How could Momma call them Miz? The mean nasty things. Why couldn't she have come inside the sweet, cool Store when we saw them breasting the hill? What did she prove? And then if they were dirty, mean and impudent, why did Momma have to call them Miz?

She stood another whole song through and then opened the screen door to look down on me crying in rage. She looked until I looked up. Her face was a brown moon that shone on me. She was beautiful. Something had happened out there, which I couldn't completely understand, but I could see that she was happy. Then she bent down and touched me as mothers of the church 'lay hands on the sick and afflicted' and I quieted.

'Go wash your face, Sister.' And she went behind the candy counter and hummed, 'Glory, glory, halle-lujah, when I lay my burden down.'

I threw the well water on my face and used the weekday handkerchief to blow my nose. Whatever the contest had been out front, I knew Momma had won.

I took the rake back to the front yard. The smudged footprints were easy to erase. I worked for a long time on my new design and laid the rake behind the wash pot. When I came back in the Store, I took Momma's hand and we both walked outside to look at the pattern.

It was a large heart with lots of hearts growing smaller inside, and piercing from the outside rim to the smallest heart was an arrow. Momma said, 'Sister, that's right pretty.' Then she turned back to the Store and resumed, 'Glory, glory, hallelujah, when I lay my burden down.'

* * *

The intensity with which young people live demands that they 'blank out' as often as possible. I didn't actually think about facing Mother until the last day of our journey. I was 'going to California'. To oranges and sunshine and movie stars and earthquakes and (finally I realised) to Mother. My old guilt came back to me like a much-missed friend. I wondered if Mr Freeman's name would be mentioned, or if I would be expected to say something about the situation myself. I certainly couldn't ask Momma, and Bailey was a zillion miles away.

The agony of wonder made the fuzzy seats hard, soured the boiled eggs, and when I looked at Momma she seemed too big and too black and very old-fashioned. Everything I saw shuttered against me. The little towns, where nobody waved, and the other passengers in the train, with whom I had achieved an almost kinfolk relationship, disappeared into a common strangeness.

I was as unprepared to meet my mother as a sinner is reluctant to meet his Maker. And all too soon she stood before me, smaller than memory would have her but more glorious than any recall. She wore a light-tan suede suit, shoes to match and a mannish hat with a feather in the band, and she patted my face with gloved hands. Except for the lipsticked mouth, white teeth and shining black eyes, she might have just emerged from a dip in a beige bath. My picture of Mother and Momma embracing on the train platform has been darkly retained through the coating of the then embarrassment and the now maturity. Mother was a blithe chick nuzzling around the large, solid dark hen. The sounds they made had a rich inner harmony. Momma's deep, slow voice lay under my mother's rapid peeps and chirps like stones under rushing water.

The younger woman kissed and laughed and rushed about collecting our coats and getting our luggage carted off. She easily took care of the details that would have demanded half of a country person's day. I was struck again by the wonder of her, and for the length of my trance, the greedy uneasiness were held at bay.

We moved into an apartment, and I slept on a sofa that miraculously transformed itself at night into a large comfortable bed. Mother stayed in Los Angeles long enough to get us settled, then she returned to San Francisco to arrange living accommodations for her abruptly enlarged family.

Momma and Bailey (he joined us a month after our arrival) and I lived in Los Angeles about six months while our permanent living arrangements were being concluded. Daddy Bailey visited occasionally, bringing shopping bags of fruit. He shone like a Sun God, benignly warming and brightening his dark subjects.

Since I was enchanted with the creation of my own world, years had to pass before I reflected on Momma's remarkable adjustment to that foreign life. An old Southern Negro woman who had lived her life under the left breast of her community learned to deal with white landlords, Mexican neighbours and Negro strangers. She shopped in supermarkets larger than the town she came from. She dealt with accents that must have struck jarringly on her ears. She, who had never been more than fifty miles from her birthplace, learned to traverse the maze of Spanish-named streets in that enigma that is Los Angeles.

She made the same kinds of friends she had always had. On late Sunday afternoons before evening church services, old women who were carbon copies of herself came to the apartment to share leftovers from the Sunday meal and religious talk of a Bright Hereafter.

When the arrangements for our move north were completed, she broke the shattering news that she was going back to Arkansas. She had done her job. She was needed by Uncle Willie. We had our own parents at last. At least we were in the same state.

There were foggy days of unknowing for Bailey and me. It was all well and good to say we would be with our parents, but after all, who were they? Would they be more severe with our didoes than she? That would be bad. Or more lax? Which would be even worse. Would we learn to speak that fast language? I doubted that, and I doubted even more that I would ever find out what they laughed about so loudly and so often.

I would have been willing to return to Stamps even without Bailey. But Momma left for Arkansas without me with her solid air packed around her like cotton.

Mother drove us towards San Francisco over the big white highway that would not have surprised me had it never ended. She talked incessantly and pointed out places of interest. As we passed Capistrano she sang a popular song that I'd heard on the radio: 'When the swallows come back to Capistrano.'

She strung humourous stories along the road like a bright wash and tried to captivate us. But her being, and her being our mother, had done the job so successfully that it was a little distracting to see her throwing good energy after good.

The big car was obedient under her one-hand driving, and she pulled on her Lucky Strike so hard that her cheeks were sucked in to make valleys in her face. Nothing could have been more magical than to have found her at last, and have her solely to ourselves in the closed world of a moving car.

Although we were both enraptured, neither Bailey nor I was unaware of her nervousness. The knowledge that we had the power to upset that goddess made us look at each other conspirationally and smile. It also made her human.

We spent a few dingy months in an Oakland apartment which had a bathtub in the kitchen and was near enough to the Southern Pacific Mole to shake

at the arrival and departure of every train. In many
ways it was St Louis revisited – along with Uncles
Tommy and Billy – and Grandmother Baxter of the
pince-nez and strict carriage was again In Residence,
though the mighty Baxter clan had fallen into hard
times after the death of Grandfather Baxter some
years earlier.

We went to school and no family member ques-
tioned the output or quality of our work. We went
to a playground which sported a basketball court, a
football field and Ping Pong tables under awnings.
On Sundays instead of going to church we went to
the movies.

I slept with Grandmother Baxter, who was afflicted
with chronic bronchitis and smoked heavily. During
the day she stubbed out half-finished cigarettes and
put them in an ashtray beside her bed. At night when
she woke up coughing she fumbled in the dark for a
butt (she called them 'Willies') and after a blaze of
light she smoked the strengthened tobacco until her
irritated throat was deadened with nicotine. For the
first weeks of sleeping with her the shaking bed and
scent of tobacco woke me, but I readily became used
to it and slept peacefully through the night.

One evening after going to bed normally, I awoke
to another kind of shaking. In the blunted light
through the window shade I saw my mother kneeling
by my bed. She brought her face close to my ear.

'Ritie,' she whispered, 'Ritie. Come, but be very
quiet.' Then she quietly rose and left the room. Duti-
fully and in a haze of ponderment I followed.
Through the half-open kitchen door the light showed
Bailey's pajamaed legs dangling from the covered

bathrub. The clock on the dining-room table said 2:30. I had never been up at that hour.

I looked Bailey a question and he returned a sheepish gaze. I knew immediately that there was nothing to fear. Then I ran my mind through the catalogue of important dates. It wasn't anybody's birthday, or April Fool's Day, or Halloween, but it was something.

Mother closed the kitchen door and told me to sit beside Bailey. She put her hands on her hips and said we had been invited to a party.

Was that enough to wake us in the middle of the night! Neither of us said anything.

She continued, 'I am giving a party and you are my honoured and only guests.'

She opened the oven and took out a pan of her crispy brown biscuits and showed us a pot of milk chocolate on the back of the stove. There was nothing for it but to laugh at our beautiful and wild mother. When Bailey and I started laughing, she joined in, except that she kept her finger in front of her mouth to try to quiet us.

We were served formally, and she apologised for having no orchestra to play for us but said she'd sing as a substitute. She sang and did the Time Step and the Snake Hips and the Suzy Q. What child can resist a mother who laughs freely and often, especially if the child's wit is mature enough to catch the sense of the joke?

Mother's beauty made her powerful and her power made her unflinchingly honest. When we asked her what she did, what her job was, she walked us to Oakland's Seventh Street, where dusty bars and smoke shops sat in the laps of storefront churches.

She pointed out Raincoat's Pinochle Parlor and Slim Jenkins' pretentious saloon. Some nights she played pinochle for money or ran a poker game at Mother Smith's or stopped at Slim's for a few drinks. She told us that she had never cheated anybody and wasn't making any preparations to do so. Her work was as honest as the job held by fat Mrs Walker (a maid), who lived next door to us, and 'a damn sight better paid'. She wouldn't bust suds for anybody nor be anyone's kitchen bitch. The good Lord gave her a mind and she intended to use it to support her mother and her children. She didn't need to ass 'And have a little fun along the way'.

In the street people were genuinely happy to see her. 'Hey, baby. What's the news?'

'Everything's steady, baby, steady.'

'How you doing, pretty?'

'I can't win, 'cause of the shape I'm in.' (Said with a laugh that belied the content.)

'Aw, they tell me the whitefolks still in the lead.' (Said as if that was not quite the whole truth.)

She supported us efficiently with humour and imagination. Occasionally we were taken to Chinese restaurants or Italian pizza parlours. We were introduced to Hungarian goulash and Irish stew. Through food we learned that there were other people in the world.

With all her jollity, Vivian Baxter had no mercy. There was a saying in Oakland at the time which, if she didn't say it herself, explained her attitude. The saying was, 'Sympathy is next to shit in the dictionary, and I can't even read.' Her temper had not diminished with the passing of time, and when a passionate nature is not eased with moments of compassion, melodrama is likely to take the stage. In each outburst of anger my mother was *fair*. She had the impartiality of nature, with the same lack of indulgence or clemency.

Before we arrived from Arkansas, an incident took place that left the main actors in jail and in the hospital. Mother had a business partner (who may have been a little more than that) with whom she ran a restaurant cum gambling casino. The partner was not shouldering his portion of the responsibility, according to Mother, and when she confronted him he became haughty and domineering, and he unforgivably called her a bitch. Now, everyone knew that although she cursed as freely as she laughed, no one cursed around her, and certainly no one cursed her. Maybe for the sake of business arrangements she restrained a spontaneous reaction. She told her partner, 'I'm going to be one bitch, and I've already been that one.' In a foolhardy gesture the man relieved himself of still another 'bitch' – and Mother shot him. She had anticipated some trouble when she determined to speak to him and so had taken the precaution to slip a little .32 in her big skirt pocket.

Shot once, the partner stumbled toward her, instead of away, and she said that since she had intended to shoot him (notice: shoot, not kill) she had no reason to run away, so she shot him a second time. It must have been a maddening situation for them. To her, each shot seemed to impel him forward, the reverse of her desire; and for him, the closer he got to her, the more she shot him. She stood her ground until he reached her and flung both arms around her neck, dragging her to the floor. She later said the police had to untwine him before he could be taken to the ambulance. And on the following day, when she was released on bail, she looked in a mirror and 'had black eyes down to here'. In throwing his arms around her, he must have struck her. She bruised easily.

The partner lived, though shot twice, and although the partnership was dissolved they retained admiration for each other. He had been shot, true, but in her fairness she had warned him. And he had had the strength to give her two black eyes and then live. Admirable qualities.

From *I Know Why the Caged Bird Sings*, published by Virago Press.

ALICE WALKER,
'IN SEARCH OF
OUR MOTHERS' GARDENS'

I described her own nature and temperament. Told
how they needed a larger life for their
expression . . . I pointed out that in lieu of proper
channels, her emotions had overflowed into paths
that dissipated them. I talked, beautifully I thought,
about an art that would be born, an art that would
open the way for women the likes of her. I asked
her to hope, and build up an inner life against the
coming of that day . . . I sang, with a strange quiver
in my voice, a promise song.

Jean Toomer, 'Avey', CANE

The poet speaking to a prostitute who falls asleep
while he's talking –

When the poet Jean Toomer walked through the

South in the early twenties, he discovered a curious thing: black women whose spirituality was so intense, so deep, so *unconscious*, that they were themselves unaware of the richness they held. They stumbled blindly through their lives: creatures so abused and mutilated in body, so dimmed and confused by pain, that they considered themselves unworthy even of hope. In the selfless abstractions their bodies became to the men who used them, they became more than 'sexual objects', more even than mere women: they became 'Saints'. Instead of being perceived as whole persons, their bodies became shrines: what was thought to be their minds became temples suitable for worship. These crazy Saints stared out at the world, wildly, like lunatics – or quietly, like suicides; and the 'God' that was in their gaze was as mute as a great stone.

Who were these Saints? These crazy, loony, pitiful women?

Some of them, without a doubt, were our mothers and grandmothers.

In the still heat of the post-Reconstruction South, this is how they seemed to Jean Toomer: exquisite butterflies trapped in an evil honey, toiling away their lives in an era, a century, that did not acknowledge them, except as 'the *mule* of the world'. They dreamed dreams that no one knew – not even themselves, in any coherent fashion – and saw visions no one could understand. They wandered or sat about the countryside crooning lullabies to ghosts, and drawing the mother of Christ in charcoal on court-house walls.

They forced their minds to desert their bodies and their striving spirits sought to rise, like frail whirlwinds from the hard red clay. And when those frail whirlwinds fell, in scattered particles, upon the ground, no one mourned. Instead, men lit candles to celebrate the emptiness that remained, as people do who enter a beautiful but vacant space to resurrect a God.

Our mothers and grandmothers, some of them: moving to music not yet written. And they waited.

They waited for a day when the unknown thing that was in them would be made known; but guessed, somehow in their darkness, that on the day of their revelation they would be long dead. Therefore to Toomer they walked, and even ran, in slow motion. For they were going nowhere immediate, and the future was not yet within their grasp. And men took our mothers and grandmothers, 'but got no pleasure from it'. So complex was their passion and their calm.

To Toomer, they lay vacant and fallow as autumn fields, with harvest time never in sight: and he saw them enter loveless marriages, without joy; and become prostitutes, without resistance; and become mothers of children, without fulfilment.

For these grandmothers and mothers of ours were not Saints, but Artists; driven to a numb and bleeding madness by the springs of creativity in them for which there was no release. They were Creators, who lived lives of spiritual waste, because they were so rich in spirituality – which is the basis of Art – that the strain of enduring their unused and unwanted talent drove them insane. Throwing away this spirituality was their pathetic attempt to lighten the soul to a weight their work-worn, sexually abused bodies could bear.

What did it mean for a black woman to be an artist in our grandmothers' time? In our great-grandmothers' day? It is a question with an answer cruel enough to stop the blood.

Did you have a genius of a great-great-grand-mother who died under some ignorant and depraved white overseer's lash? Or was she required to bake biscuits for a lazy backwater tramp, when she cried out in her soul to paint watercolours of sunsets, or the rain falling on the green and peaceful pasture-lands? Or was her body broken and forced to bear children (who were more often than not sold away from her) — eight, ten, fifteen, twenty children — when her one joy was the thought of modelling heroic figures of rebellion, in stone or clay?

How was the creativity of the black woman kept alive, year after year and century after century, when for most of the years black people have been in America, it was a punishable crime for a black person to read or write? And the freedom to paint, to sculpt, to expand the mind with action did not exist. Consider, if you can bear to imagine it, what might have been the result if singing, too, had been forbid-den by law. Listen to the voices of Bessie Smith, Billie Holiday, Nina Simone, Roberta Flack and Aretha Franklin, among others, and imagine those voices muzzled for life. Then you may begin to comprehend the lives of our 'crazy', 'Sainted' mothers and grand-mothers. The agony of the lives of women who might have been Poets, Novelists, Essayists and Short-Story Writers (over a period of centuries), who died with their real gifts stifled within them.

And, if this were the end of the story, we would have cause to cry out in my paraphrase of Okot p'Bitek's great poem:

O, my clanswomen
Let us all cry together!
Come,
Let us mourn the death of our mother,
The death of a Queen
The ash that was produced
By a great fire!
O, this homestead is utterly dead
Close the gates
With *lacari* thorns,
For our mother
The creator of the Stool is lost!
And all the young women
Have perished in the wilderness!

But this is not the end of the story, for all the young women — our mothers and grandmothers, *ourselves* — have not perished in the wilderness. And if we ask ourselves why, and search for and find the answer, we will know beyond all efforts to erase it from our minds, just exactly who, and of what, we black American women are.

One example, perhaps the most pathetic, most misunderstood one, can provide a backdrop for our mothers' work: Phillis Wheatley, a slave in the 1700s.

Virginia Woolf, in her book *A Room of One's Own*, wrote that in order for a woman to write fiction she must have two things, certainly: a room of her own (with key and lock) and enough money to support herself.

What then are we to make of Phillis Wheatley, a slave, who owned not even herself? This sickly, frail black girl who required a servant of her own at times — her health was so precarious — and who, had she been white, would have been easily considered the intellectual superior of all the women and most of the men in the society of her day.

Virginia Woolf wrote further, speaking of course not of our Phillis, that 'any woman born with a great gift in the sixteenth century [insert 'eighteenth century', insert 'black woman', insert 'born or made a slave'] would certainly have gone crazed, shot herself, or ended her days in some lonely cottage outside the village, half witch, half wizard [insert 'Saint'], feared and mocked at. For it needs little skill and psychology to be sure that a highly gifted girl who had tried to use her gift for poetry would have been so thwarted and hindered by contrary instincts [add 'chains, guns, the lash, the ownership of one's body by someone else, submission to an alien religion'], that she must have lost her health and sanity to a certainty.'

They key words, as they relate to Phillis, are 'contrary instincts'. For when we read the poetry of Phillis Wheatley – as when we read the novels of Nella Larsen or the oddly false-sounding autobiography of that freest of all black women writers, Zora Hurston – evidence of 'contrary instincts' is everywhere. Her loyalties were completely divided, as was, without question, her mind.

But how could this be otherwise? Captured at seven, a slave of wealthy, doting whites who instilled in her the 'savagery' of the Africa they 'rescued' her from . . . one wonders if she was even able to remember her homeland as she had known it, or as it really was.

Yet, because she did try to use her gift for poetry in a world that made her a slave, she was 'so thwarted and hindered by . . . contrary instincts, that she . . . lost her health . . .' In the last years of her brief life, burdened not only with the need to express her gift but also with a penniless, friendless 'freedom' and several small children for whom she was forced to do strenuous work to feed, she lost her health, certainly. Suffering from malnutrition and neglect and who knows what mental agonies, Phillis Wheatley died.

So torn by 'contrary instincts' was black, kid-napped, enslaved Phillis that her description of 'the Goddess' — as she poetically called the Liberty she did not have — is ironically, cruelly humorous. And, in fact, has held Phillis up to ridicule for more than a century. It is usually read prior to hanging Phillis's memory as that of a fool. She wrote:

> The Goddess comes, she moves divinely fair,
> Olive and laurel binds her *golden* hair.
> Wherever shines this native of the skies,
> Unnumber'd charms and recent graces rise.
> [My italics]

It is obvious that Phillis, the slave, combed the 'Goddess's' hair every morning; prior, perhaps, to bringing in the milk, or fixing her mistress's lunch. She took her imagery from the one thing she saw elevated above all others.

With the benefit of hindsight we ask, 'How could she?'

But at last, Phillis, we understand. No more snick-ering when your stiff, struggling, ambivalent lines are forced on us. We know now that you were not an idiot or a traitor, only a sickly little black girl, snatched from your home and country and made a slave; a woman who still struggled to sing the song that was your gift, although in a land of barbarians who praised you for your bewildered tongue. It is not so much what you sang, as that you kept alive, in so many of our ancestors, *the notion of song*.

Black women are called, in the folklore that so aptly identifies one's status in society, 'the *mule* of the world', because we have been handed the burdens that everyone else – *everyone* else – refused to carry. We have also been called 'Matriarchs', 'Superwomen', and 'Mean and Evil Bitches'. Not to mention 'Castraters' and 'Sapphire's Mama'. When we have pleaded for understanding, our character has been distorted; when we have asked for simple caring, we have been handed empty inspirational appelations, then stuck in the farthest corner. When we have asked for love, we have been given children. In short, even our plainer gifts, our labours of fidelity and love, have been knocked down our throats. To be an artist and a black woman, even today, lowers our status in many respects, rather than raises it: and yet, artists we will be.

Therefore we must fearlessly pull out of ourselves and look at and identify with our lives the living creativity some of our great-grandmothers were not allowed to know. I stress *some* of them because it is well known that the majority of our great-grandmothers knew, even without 'knowing' it, the reality of their spirituality, even if they didn't recognise it beyond what happened in the singing at church – and they never had any intention of giving it up.

How they did it – those millions of black women

who were not Phillis Wheatley, or Lucy Terry or Frances Harper or Zora Hurston or Nella Larsen or Bessie Smith; or Elizabeth Catlett, or Katherine Dunham, either – brings me to the title of this essay, 'In Search of Our Mothers' Gardens', which is a personal account that is yet shared, in its theme and its meaning, by all of us. I found, while thinking about the far-reaching world of the creative black woman, that often the truest answer to a question that really matters can be found very close.

In the late 1920s my mother ran away from home to marry my father. Marriage, if not running away, was expected of seventeen-year-old girls. By the time she was twenty, she had two children and was pregnant with a third. Five children later, I was born. And this is how I came to know my mother: she seemed a large, soft, loving-eyed woman who was rarely impatient in our home. Her quick, violent temper was on view only a few times a year, when she battled with the white landlord who had the misfortune to suggest to her that her children did not need to go to school.

She made all the clothes we wore, even my brother's overalls. She made all the towels and sheets we used. She spent the summers canning vegetables and fruits. She spent the winter evenings making quilts enough to cover all our beds.

During the 'working' day, she laboured beside – not behind – my father in the fields. Her day began before sun-up, and did not end until late at night. There was never a moment for her to sit down, undisturbed, to unravel her own private thoughts; never a time free from interruption – by work or the noisy inquiries of her many children. And yet, it is to my mother – and all our mothers who were not famous – that I went in search of the secret of what has fed that muzzled and often mutilated, but vibrant, creative spirit that the black woman has inherited, and that pops out in wild and unlikely places to this day.

But when, you will ask, did my overworked mother have time to know or care about feeding the creative spirit?

The answer is so simple that many of us have spent years discovering it. We have constantly looked high, when we should have looked high – and low.

For example: in the Smithsonian Institution in Washington, DC, there hangs a quilt unlike any other in the world. In fanciful, inspired, and yet simple and identifiable figures, it portrays the story of the Crucifixion. It is considered rare, beyond price. Though it follows no known pattern of quilt-making, and though it is made of bits and pieces of worthless rags, it is obviously the work of a person of powerful imagination and deep spiritual feeling. Below this quilt I saw a note that says it was made by 'an anonymous Black woman in Alabama, a hundred years ago'.

If we could locate this 'anonymous' black woman from Alabama, she would turn out to be one of our grandmothers – an artist who left her mark in the only materials she could afford, and in the only medium her position in society allowed her to use.

As Virginia Woolf wrote further, in *A Room of One's Own*:

Yet genius of a sort must have existed among

women as it must have existed among the working class. [Change this to 'slaves' and 'the wives and daughters of sharecroppers'.] Now and again an Emily Brontë or a Robert Burns [change this to 'a Zora Hurston or a Richard Wright'] blazes out and proves its presence. But certainly it never got itself on to paper. When, however, one reads of a witch being ducked, of a woman possessed by devils [or 'Sainthood'], of a wise woman selling herbs [our root workers], or even a very remarkable man who had a mother, then I think we are on the track of a lost novelist, a suppressed poet, of some mute and inglorious Jane Austen . . . Indeed, I would venture to guess that Anon, who wrote so many poems without singing them, was often a woman . . .

And so our mothers and grandmothers have, more often than not anonymously, handed on the creative spark, the seed of the flower they themselves never hoped to see: or like a sealed letter they could not plainly read.

And so it is, certainly, with my own mother. Unlike 'Ma' Rainey's songs, which retained their creator's name even while blasting forth from Bessie Smith's mouth, no song or poem will bear my mother's name. Yet so many of the stories that I write, that we all write, are my mother's stories. Only recently did I fully realise this: that through years of listening to my mother's stories of her life, I have absorbed not only the stories themselves, but something of the manner in which she spoke, something of the urgency that involves the knowledge that her stories – like her life – must be recorded. It is probably for this reason that so much of what I have written is about characters whose counterparts in real life are so much older than I am.

But the telling of these stories, which came from my mother's lips as naturally as breathing, was not the only way my mother showed herself as an artist. For stories, too, were subject to being distracted, to dying without conclusion. Dinners must be started, and cotton must be gathered before the big rains. The artist that was and is my mother showed itself to me only after many years. This is what I finally· noticed.·

Like Mem, a character in *The Third Life of Grange Copeland*, my mother adorned with flowers whatever shabby house we were forced to live in. And not just your typical straggly country stand of zinnias, either. She planted ambitious gardens – and still does – with over fifty different varieties of plants that bloom profusely from early March until late November. Before she left home for the fields, she watered her flowers, chopped up the grass, and laid out new beds. When she returned from the fields she might divide clumps of bulbs, dig a cold pit, uproot and replant roses, or prune branches from her taller bushes or trees – until night came and it was too dark to see.

Whatever she planted grew as if by magic, and her fame as a grower of flowers spread over three counties. Because of her creativity with her flowers, even my memories of poverty are seen through a screen of blooms – sunflowers, petunias, roses, dahlias, forsythia, spirea, delphiniums, verbena . . . and on and on.

And I remember people coming to my mother's yard to be given cuttings from her flowers; I hear again the praise showered on her because whatever rocky soil she landed on, she turned into a garden. A garden so brilliant with colours, so original in its design, so magnificent with life and creativity, that to this day people drive by our house in Georgia – perfect strangers and imperfect strangers – and ask to stand or walk among my mother's art.

I notice that it is only when my mother is working in her flowers that she is radiant, almost to the point of being invisible – except as Creator: hand and eye. She is involved in work her soul must have. Ordering the universe in the image of her personal conception of Beauty.

Her face, as she prepares the Art that is her gift, is a legacy of respect she leaves to me, for all that illuminates and cherishes life. She has handed down respect for the possibilities – and the will to grasp them.

For her, so hindered and intruded upon in so many ways, being an artist has still been a daily part of her life. This ability to hold on, even in very simple ways, is work black women have done for a very long time.

This poem is not enough, but it is something, for the woman who literally covered the holes in our walls with sunflowers:

> They were women then
> My mama's generation
> Husky of voice – Stout of
> Step
> With fists as well as
> Hands
> How they battered down
> Doors

And ironed
Starched white
Shirts
How they led
Armies
Headragged Generals
Across mined
Fields
Booby-trapped
Kitchens
To discover books
Desks
A place for us
How they knew what we
Must know
Without knowing a page
Of it
Themselves.

Guided by my heritage of a love of beauty and a respect for strength – in search of my mother's garden, I found my own.

And perhaps in Africa over two hundred years ago, there was just such a mother, perhaps she painted vivid and daring decorations in oranges and yellows and greens on the walls of her hut; perhaps she sang – in a voice like Roberta Flack's – *sweetly* over the compounds of her village; perhaps she wove the most stunning mats or told the most ingenious stories of all the village storytellers. Perhaps she was herself a poet – though only her daughter's name is signed to the poems that we know.

Perhaps Phillis Wheatley's mother was also an artist.

Perhaps in more than Phillis Wheatley's biological life is her mother's signature made clear.

From *In Search of Our Mothers' Gardens*, published by The Women's Press.

MARGE PIERCY,
'CRESCENT MOON
LIKE A CANOE'

This month you carried me late and heavy
in your belly and finally near Tuesday
midnight you gave me light and life, the season
Kore returns to Demeter, and you suffer
and I cannot save you though I burn with dreams.

Memories the colour of old blood,
scraps of velvet gowns, lace, chiffon veils,
your sister's stage costumes (Ziegfeld
didn't stint) we fingered together, you
padding in sneakers and wash-worn housedresses.

You grew celery by tucking sliced off
bottoms in the soil. You kept a compost
pile in 1940. Your tomatoes glowed
like traffic signals in the table-sized yard.
Don't kill spiders, you warned.

In an asbestos box in Detroit where sputtering
factories yellow the air, where sheets
on the line turn ashen, you nurtured
a backyard jungle. Every hungry cat
wanted to enter and every child.

You who had not been allowed to finish
tenth grade but sent to be a frightened
chambermaid, carried home every week
armloads of books from the library
rummaging them late at night, insomniac,

riffling the books like boxes of chocolates
searching for the candied cherries, the nuts,
hunting for the secrets, the formulae,
the knowledge those others learned
that made them shine and never ache.

You were taught to feel stupid; you
were made to feel dirty; you were
forced to feel helpless; you were trained
to feel lost, uprooted, terrified.
You could not love yourself or me.

Dreamer of fables that hid their own
endings, kitchen witch, reader of palms,
you gave me gifts and took them back
but the real ones boil in the blood
and swell in the breasts, furtive, strong.

You gave me hands that can pick up
a wild bird so that the bird relaxes,
turns and stares. I have handled

fifty stunned and injured birds and killed
only two through clumsiness, with your touch.

You taught me to see the scale on the bird
leg, the old woman's scalp pink as a rose
under the fluff, the golden flecks in the iris
of your eye, the silver underside of leaves
blown back. I am your poet, mother.

You did not want the daughter you got.
You wanted a girl to flirt as you did
and marry as you had and chew the same
sour coughed up cud, yet you wanted too
to birth a witch, a revenger, a sword

of hearts who would do all the things
you feared. Don't do it, they'll kill
you, you're bad, you said, slapping me down
hard but always you whispered, I could have!
Only rebellion flashes like lightning.

I wanted to take you with me, you don't
remember. We fought like snakes, biting
hard at each other's spine to snap free.
You burned my paper armour, rifled my diaries,
snuffed my panties looking for smudge of sex,

so I took off and never came back. You can't
imagine how I still long to save you,
to carry you off, who can't trust me
to make coffee, but your life and mine pass
in different centuries, under altered suns.

I see your blood soaking into the linoleum,
I see you twisted, a mop some giant hand
is wringing out. Pain in the careless joke
and shouted insult and knotted fist. Pain like knives
and forks set out on the domestic table.

You look to men for salvation and every year
finds you more helpless. Do I battle
for other women, myself included,
because I cannot give you anything
you want? I cannot midwife you free.

In my childhood bed we float, your sweet
husky voice singing about the crescent
moon, with two horns sharp and bright we would
climb into like a boat and row away
and see, you sang, where the pretty moon goes.

In the land where the moon hides, mothers
and daughters hold each other tenderly.
There is no male law at five o'clock.
Our sameness and our difference do not clash
metal on metal but we celebrate and learn.

My muse, your voice on the phone wavers with
   tears.
The life you gave me burns its acetylene
of buried anger, unused talents, rotted wishes,
the compost of discontent, flaring into words
strong for other women under your waning moon.

'Crescent moon like a canoe' is from Marge Piercy's
collection, *Eight Chambers*, published by Alfred A
Knopf, USA.

CONTRIBUTORS' NOTES

Maya Angelou was born in 1928 in St Louis, Missouri. After the break-up of her parents' marriage she and her brother Bailey went to live with their grandmother, whose general store was the centre of life for the black community in Stamps, Arkansas. At sixteen, having just graduated from school, Maya gave birth to her son, Guy.

In the years that followed she was a waitress, singer, actress, dancer, black activist, editor, as well as mother. In her twenties she toured Europe and Africa in *Porgy and Bess*. Moving to New York, she joined the Harlem Writers' Guild while continuing to earn her living as a nightclub singer and performer in Genet's *The Blacks*. She became involved in black struggles in the 1960s and then spent several years in Ghana as editor of *African Review*.

Maya Angelou's five books of autobiography: *I Know Why The Caged Bird Sings, Gather Together In My Name, Singin' and Swingin' And Gettin' Merry Like*

Christmas, The Heart Of A Woman, All God's Children Need Travelling Shoes, are a testament to the talents and resilience of this extraordinary writer.

Rachel Barton was born in Merseyside in a middle-class, suburban family. She has worked as a lecturer in higher education in London and has since lived in different cities in Britain.

Catherine Cookson was born in Tyne Dock, the illegitimate daughter of a poverty-stricken woman, Kate, whom she believed to be her older sister. She began work in service but eventually moved south to Hastings where she met and married a local grammar school master.

Mrs Cookson published her first novel at the age of forty-four, in 1950. Since then she has written in excess of eighty works of fiction, including ten books for children. Mrs Cookson now outsells Agatha Christie; worldwide sales figures are over eighty-five million copies with over forty million sold in English paperback alone. Her books have been translated into fourteen languages.

Televised works include *The Mallens*, a six-part series screened on ITV in the 1970s; *The Fifteen Streets*, a TV movie made by Tyne Tees and World-wide Television, which was nominated for an Emmy Award in 1990; *The Black Candle* and *The Black Velvet Gown*, which won the 1991 Emmy Award for the Best International Television Drama. Each of these films achieved audience ratings of between ten and thirteen million viewers.

Mrs Cookson is now eighty-seven and lives with her husband in Newcastle. During her career she has been awarded an OBE, and an honorary MA and this year a D.Litt. by Sunderland Polytechnic. In 1993 she was made a Dame in the New Year's Honours List in recognition of her work for charity.

Mary Daly describes herself as a Voyager, moving beyond the imprisoning mental, physical, emotional, spiritual walls of the State of Possession; a Positively Revolting Hag, repelling the forces of patriarchy; and a Crafty Pirate, Righteously Plundering treasures of knowledge that have been stolen and hidden from women and struggling to Smuggle these back in such a way that they can be seen as distinct from their mindbinding trappings.

She holds three doctorates, including doctorates in theology and philosophy from the University of Fribourg, Switzerland. An associate professor of theology at Boston College, she is the author of *Beyond God the Father, Gyn/Ecology, Pure Lust, Websters' First New Intergalactic Wickedary of the English Language*, Conjured in Cahoots with Jane Caputi, and *Outercourse/The Be-Dazzling Voyage/Containing Recollections from My* Logbook of A Radical Feminist Philosopher/(*Be-ing an Account of My Time/Space Travels and Ideas/ − Then, Again, Now and How*) (all published by The Women's Press), and *The Church and the Second Sex*.

Stephanie Dowrick is a writer, psychotherapist, publisher and mother of Gabriel (aged ten) and Kezia (aged nine). In addition to her novel, *Running Backwards Over Sand*, her work includes the international non-fiction bestsellers *Intimacy and Solitude* and *The*

Intimacy and Solitude Self-Therapy Book, both published by The Women's Press.

She was a founder of The Women's Press in 1977 and was Managing Director until 1983. In 1991 she was appointed Chairwoman of The Women's Press.

Born in New Zealand, Stephanie Dowrick lived in Europe for much of her adult life and is now based in Sydney, Australia.

Marilyn French received her doctorate from Harvard University in 1972. Her three novels, *The Women's Room* (1977), *The Bleeding Heart* (1980) and *Her Mother's Daughter* (1987) are international bestsellers and feminist classics. She has also written *The War Against Women, Beyond Power: On Women, Men and Morals* (1985) and *Shakespeare's Division Of Experience* (1981). Born in New York City, she now divides her time between New York and Florida.

Kate prefers to remain anonymous.

Audre Lorde (1934–1992) described herself as a black lesbian, poet, mother and warrior woman. She published eight collections of poetry and five volumes of prose, which include *The Black Unicorn, Chosen Poems – Old and New, Sister Outsider, The Cancer Journals* and *A Burst Of Light*. At the time of her death, after a battle with cancer which lasted fourteen years, she was the New York State Poet.

Marge Piercy is the major bestselling author of thirteen novels including the universally acclaimed *Woman on the Edge of Time* (The Women's Press, 1979), as well as the astounding *Vida* (The Women's

Press, 1980), *The High Cost of Living* (The Women's Press, 1979), *Braided Lives* (1982), *Fly Away Home* (1984), *Gone to Soldiers* (1988), *Summer People* (1989), *Body of Glass* (1992) which won the Arthur C Clarke Award for Best Science Fiction published in the United Kingdom in 1992, and *The Longings of Women* (1994). She has published 13 volumes of poetry in the States. Her selected poems, *The Eight Chambers of the Heart*, is being published by Michael Joseph/Penguin.

Sylvia Plath was born in Boston, Massachusetts in 1932. She went to Smith College, Massachusetts and Newnham College, Cambridge and in 1956 she married Ted Hughes. In 1959 the Hughes moved permanently to England, settling in Devon in 1961. Her first volume of poetry, *The Colossus*, appeared in 1960 and in 1963 her only novel *The Bell Jar* was published. Less than a month after its publication Sylvia Plath, separated from Ted Hughes, committed suicide. She left two children. *Ariel*, her best known collection of poetry, was published in 1965.

George Sand (pseudonym of Amandine–Aurore Lucille Dupin, Baronne Dudevant) was born in 1804. In 1831 she separated from her husband Baron Dudevant and went to Paris to begin a life as an independent writer. Her novels include *Indiana* (1832), *Lélia* (1833), *Jacques* (1834), *La Mare au diable* (1846), *La Petite Fadette* (1848) and *François le champi* (1850). *Histoire de ma vie* (1854–1855) is her autobiography. George Sand died in 1876.

May Sarton is an internationally acclaimed poet and

novelist. Her much-loved series of autobiographical works include: *Journal Of A Solitude*, *After the Stroke* and *Encore* all published by The Women's Press. The Women's Press also publish May Sarton's novels: *As We Are Now*, *A Reckoning*, *The Magnificent Spinster*, *The Education of Harriet Hatfield*, *Mrs Stevens Hears the Mermaids Singing* and her personally selected volume of poetry, *Halfway to Silence*.

May Sarton was born in Europe, but for most of her life has made the East Coast of America her home.

Alice Walker was born in Eatonton, Georgia. She has received many awards, including The Radcliffe Fellowship and a Guggenheim Fellowship. Her hugely popular novel, *The Color Purple*, won the American Book Award, plus the Pulitzer Prize for Fiction in 1983, and was subsequently made into an internationally successful film by Steven Spielberg.

The Temple of My Familiar was published in 1989 and was a bestseller. (It appeared on the *New York Times* bestseller list for four months.) Alice Walker is the author of two other novels, *The Third Life of Grange Copeland* (1970) and *Meridian* (1976), of which C L R James said 'I have not read a novel superior to this', two books of essays and memoirs, *In Search of Our Mothers' Gardens: Womanist Prose* and *Living by the Word*; plus two short story collections, *You Can't Keep a Good Woman Down* and *In Love and Trouble*, all published by The Women's Press. Her latest novel *Possessing the Secret of Joy* was published in 1992.

Alice Walker has published several volumes of poetry, *Good Night Willie Lee, I'll See You in the Morning*, *Horses Make a Landscape More Beautiful*, *Once* and *Revolutionary Petunias*, and her complete poems are published in the volume *Her Blue Body Everything We Know: Earthling Poems 1965–1990*. Her book, *Warrior Marks* (with Pratibha Parmar, 1993), details the making of the acclaimed film of the same name, which campaigns for an end to female genital mutilation.

Virginia Woolf was born in London in 1882. She was educated at home and in 1904, at the age of twenty-two, she began a career in literary journalism. Her first novel, *The Voyage Out*, appeared in 1915, and her subsequent works include *Mrs Dalloway* (1925), *To the Lighthouse* (1927) and *The Waves* (1931). Her last novel, *Between The Acts*, was published after her death, at the age of fifty-nine, in 1941.

Virginia Woolf wrote two major non-fiction works, *A Room Of One's Own* (1929) and *Three Guineas* (1938), and her interest in biography is shown in her life of the art critic Roger Fry (1940) and in the highly fictionalised account of Vita Sackville-West's life which forms the basis of *Orlando* (1928).

In 1912 she married Leonard Woolf and in 1917 they founded The Hogarth Press, which published the early work of writers such as T S Eliot, Katherine Mansfield and Sigmund Freud.

The Women's Press is Britain's leading women's publishing house. Established in 1978, we publish high-quality fiction and non-fiction from outstanding women writers worldwide. Our exciting and diverse list includes literary fiction, detective novels, biography and autobiography, health, women's studies, handbooks, literary criticism, psychology and self help, the arts, our popular Livewire Books series for young women and the bestselling annual *Women Artists Diary* featuring beautiful colour and black-and-white illustrations from the best in contemporary women's art.

If you would like more information about our books or about our mail order book club, please send an A5 sae for our latest catalogue and complete list to:

The Sales Department
The Women's Press Ltd
34 Great Sutton Street
London EC1V 0DX
Tel: 0171 251 3007
Fax: 0171 608 1938